剑桥双语分级阅读·小说馆（第2版）

■ 原版系列编辑　Phil

U0681018

The Lady in White 神秘搭车人

[英] 科林·坎贝尔　著

王　欢　编译

北京语言大学出版社
BEIJING LANGUAGE AND CULTURE
UNIVERSITY PRESS

CAMBRIDGE
UNIVERSITY PRESS

社图号25018

This is a bilingual English-simplified Chinese edition of the following title originally published by Cambridge University Press & Assessment:

The Lady in White Level 4 (ISBN: 9780521666206) © Cambridge University Press & Assessment 1999

This bilingual English-simplified Chinese edition for the People's Republic of China is published by arrangement with The Chancellor, Masters, and Scholars of the University of Cambridge, acting through its department Cambridge University Press & Assessment, Cambridge, United Kingdom.

This edition © Beijing Language and Culture University Press 2025 is published under licence.

This bilingual English-simplified Chinese edition is authorised for sale in the People's Republic of China (excluding Hong Kong SAR, Macao SAR and Taiwan Province) only. Unauthorised export of this bilingual English-simplified Chinese edition is a violation of the Copyright Act. No part of this publication may be reproduced or distributed by any means, or stored in a database or retrieval system, without the prior written permission of Cambridge University Press & Assessment and Beijing Language and Culture University Press.

本双语版仅限在中华人民共和国境内销售。本书任何部分之文字及图片，如未获得出版者书面同意，不得用任何方式抄袭、节录或翻印。

北京市版权局著作权合同登记图字：01-2024-3256号

图书在版编目（CIP）数据

神秘搭车人：英汉对照 ／（英）科林·坎贝尔
(Colin Campbell) 著；王欢编译. -- 2版. -- 北京：
北京语言大学出版社，2025. 3. --（剑桥双语分级阅读
小说馆）. -- ISBN 978-7-5619-6737-9

Ⅰ. H319. 4

中国国家版本馆CIP数据核字第202595U4P4号

神秘搭车人
SHENMI DACHEREN

责任编辑：李　珍
责任印制：周　燚

出版发行：北京语言大学出版社
社　　址：北京市海淀区学院路 15 号，100083
网　　址：www.blcup.com
电子信箱：service@blcup.com
电　　话：编 辑 部 010-8230 1019
　　　　　发 行 部 010-8230 3650/3591/3648
　　　　　北语书店 010-8230 3653
　　　　　网购咨询 010-8230 3908
印　　刷：东港股份有限公司
版　　次：2017 年 6 月第 1 版　2025 年 3 月第 2 版　印　次：2025 年 3 月第 1 次印刷
开　　本：880 毫米 × 1230 毫米　1/32　　印　张：6.125
字　　数：147 千字　　　　　　　　　　　　　定　价：23.00 元

PRINTED IN CHINA
凡有印装质量问题，本社负责调换。售后QQ号1367565611，电话010-82303590

Preface

前言

　　"剑桥双语分级阅读·小说馆"是一套从剑桥大学出版社引进的面向非英语国家英语学习者的分级系列读物，由英语语言教学专家及小说作家合力创作。创作过程历时三十余年，出版后受到世界各地英语教师和英语学习者的喜爱，许多读本再版多次，三十余年来畅销不衰，成为受全球英语学习者青睐的优秀读本。

　　本系列读物具有以下突出特色：

　　1. 是原创英语读物，而非改编自普通作品的读物。因此，阅读本系列读物，我们读到的是原汁原味的原创英语，而非人为改编过的二手英语。

　　2. 是当代优秀短篇小说，而非年代久远的小说。因此，阅读本系列读物，我们读到的是当今鲜活的、学了就能用的英语，而非穿越时空的、学了用不上的英语；了解的是与读者同时代不同国家人们的生活和思想，而非隔代人的生活、文化和风土人情。

　　3. 是专为非英语国家的英语学习者量身定制的读物，而非为英语母语者所写的大众读物。因此，本系列读物是中国读者首选的英语学习读物。

　　4. 是英美知名小说家和英语语言教学专家合力创作的读物。小说家保障了读物的可读性与可欣赏性，英语语言教学专家保障了读物语言作为英语习得材料的科学性与可学性。本系列读物中的多个读本都曾在世界上颇具影响力的"语言学习者文学奖"（Language Learner Literature Award）评选中获得大奖。因此，阅读本系列读物，我们会在欣赏小说的同时，自然而然地、有效地提高自己的英语水平。

5. 本系列读物的故事题材丰富多样，包括侦探、情感、历险、悬疑、人文、科幻、喜剧等，读者可以随心选择自己喜欢的类别阅读；故事内容生动有趣，故事情节引人入胜、扣人心弦，读者一旦开始阅读，就想一口气读完，使阅读真正升华到"悦读"。

6. 随书附赠的音频材料内容精彩，是专业配音员的演绎再创作。听着它，我们犹如在听广播剧、听评书，又仿佛是在听电影、听话剧……这种聆听英语的享受将彻底扫除学生对英语听力的畏难心理。

7. 本系列读物所使用的语言，既有英式英语，也有美式英语，对应的音频材料也相应分为英音和美音，读者可根据自己的喜好来选择。

8. 本系列近百本读物根据《欧洲语言共同参考框架》(CEFR) 和剑桥大学外语考评部开发的 ESOL 考试的标准来确定级别划分，是建立在科学研究和实践基础之上的分级。全套共分七个级别（与中国学生英语基础水平的大致对应关系，请参见图书封底表格），读者可根据自己的英语基础选择相应级别的读本来学习。

为了更好地帮助中国学生学习和欣赏，"剑桥双语分级阅读·小说馆"从剑桥大学出版社原版引进后又增加了以下内容：

1. 增加了适量的辅助学习内容，包括"读前思考""读后活动""学习指导"三个板块，其中"学习指导"板块又包括生词、短语和表达、文化点滴、阅读练习四项内容。增加这些板块的目的是全方位帮助学生提升英语阅读能力，扩充词汇量，扫除阅读中的文化障碍，增强对英语小说的鉴赏能力。

2. 增加了小说全文的参考译文。出于语言学习的考虑，译文多采用直译，但也尽量符合中文的表达习惯。

值得一提的是，所增加的辅助学习内容和参考译文，全部由来自全国不同省市知名中学（包括人大附中、北大附中、清华附中、黄冈中学、上海中学等三十余所中学）的一线英语教师完成。这些一线教师的加盟，确保了所加内容与中国学生的英语学习特点和学习需求相吻合，为学生阅读和欣赏读物、提高英语水平给予恰到好处的助力。

英语阅读是英语课堂的延伸和补充，也是培养英语语感、提高英语水平的有效途径。选择一套好的英语读物，收获的将不仅仅是语言的进步。欢迎年轻朋友们来到"剑桥双语分级阅读·小说馆"，打开一本本好书，品味一个个好故事，为实现梦想搭建桥梁。

北京语言大学出版社

Contents 目录

People in the story

故事中的人物

John: a successful television producer.
约翰是一个成功的电视节目制作人。

Jenny: John's assistant.
珍妮是约翰的助理。

Rachel: John's wife.
雷切尔是约翰的妻子。

Patrick: the young son of Rachel and John.
帕特里克是雷切尔和约翰年幼的儿子。

Mrs Reagan: the woman from the pub on Inishbofin.

里根夫人是伊尼什博芬岛上酒吧里的一个女人。

A policeman.

一个警察。

The man who gives the hitch-hiker a lift.

一个给搭便车者提供便车的男人。

The lady in white.

白衣女人。

Before reading

读前思考

1. Look at the front cover and read the back cover blurb. What do you think the book is about?

2. Look at the list of characters on pages 2 and 3. What do you think is going to happen in the story?

3. Match the chapter titles with the sentences from each chapter.

Chapter 1 Light and darkness

Chapter 2 Happy birthday

Chapter 3 The lady in white

Chapter 4 Losing control

a) 'I turned to look at her for a moment and noticed her face was wet, and her hair, and her dress.'

b) She had never seen him like this. He sat there in his own world and she was afraid to ask him any more questions.

c) 'I mean, this is a special day, for him, for all of us, and I just wanted to do something special...'

d) It was strange, John thought, to feel so successful and so worried at the same time.

4. If you have the recording, listen to Chapter 1.

Chapter 1
Light and darkness

The man and the woman danced around the office holding each other. They smiled and laughed as they danced. They had their arms around each other. They danced and they danced. They did not want this moment to go away.

'We did it, John. We really did it.'

'I know we did, Jenny. I know.'

John was a television producer and Jenny was his assistant. They were getting excited about a series of six television programmes they had made. The series was called *Know Your Mind, Love Your Body.* It was about the relationship between the body and the mind. Each programme had looked at a different subject: other forms of medicine, meditation, yoga, a good diet and so on. It had not been an expensive series to make, but millions of people had watched it and the newspapers had talked a lot about it.

It had been John's idea. He felt there was a growing interest in the subject, but even he had been surprised by the size of the audiences and the interest in the newspapers.

'Tell me again what the boss said, John.'

'He said he thinks it's the best series he's seen since...ever. And he talked about how much the newspapers loved the programmes. Our managing director is a very, very happy man. He wants to talk to me about money, about my salary, about giving me a rise, would you believe?'

The smile disappeared from Jenny's face for a second when he talked about his salary.

'And a rise for you too, of course!' John added. Jenny's smile returned. 'He thinks it might win the Montreux Gold Prize for best documentary programme.'

'It's fantastic,' said Jenny. 'We did it. It's a success. We really did it.' Jenny was dancing by herself now.

'Of course it's successful,' John joked. 'We believed it would be successful, and it is successful. If you believe in something, it will happen. It may not happen exactly the way you want, but it will happen. If we believe that something is true, it becomes true. That's what the programmes were all about.'

'Have you talked to Rachel yet?' Jenny asked, bringing him back to the present.

'I haven't had a chance to phone Rachel yet. I've just got off the phone with the managing director; I haven't had a chance. I'll do it now. But listen, let's talk over lunch. I have an idea for another programme.'

Rachel was John's wife. She was the first person he always ran to talk to when he had good news, or bad news, or no news, or when he felt low, or when he felt good. They had been married for just under two years and in that time they had kept no secrets from each other. They told each other everything. It was why their relationship was so good, so strong. They discussed how they felt, what they were thinking, what they had done. Everything. They had no secrets from each other.

He picked up the phone and turned his back on Jenny before she had even moved towards the door, but she didn't mind. Jenny knew him, she knew his love for his wife and son, she knew how excited he was. She left the room smiling to herself. All days should be like this, she thought. But no, then they wouldn't be special, and this was a special day.

John sat down at his desk with the phone in his hand. He looked happily around his office and out of the window. The views from his fourth-floor office were some of the best in London: The Houses of Parliament were to the west, Tower Bridge was so close you could imagine reaching out and touching it and the whole building overlooked the River Thames. The river was busy today; there were boats carrying tourists, and office workers having a birthday party on a hired pleasure boat. Even the river police looked relaxed today as they went up and down the river doing work that was often unpleasant.

John almost never took time to look out of the window. He sometimes asked himself why the television company had spent so much money on a building in this beautiful but expensive part of London. Everyone who worked in the building was either out making films or so busy in meetings that they never looked out to enjoy the view.

Probably the building with its views was for the visitors from other British and foreign television companies who came to buy their programmes. It was big, big money, and the least you could do for these important men and women was offer them such a view. Maybe it helped sell the programmes, especially on a beautiful spring morning like this.

At this moment, John felt very good about himself as he looked at his office, as he thought about the success of his programmes. But then he remembered the phone in his hand and that he wanted to talk to Rachel. He paused and put the phone down again.

John was worried about Rachel. She had not seemed happy for the last couple of weeks. She had seemed nervous, worried about something. Worried most of all about Patrick, their young son. She had not wanted to go out anywhere recently. He had gone out alone at least three times in the last two weeks. To a party, to a play, to dinner with friends. The kind of thing that Rachel loved. But she had not wanted to go out of the house. She had not wanted to leave Patrick.

Twice she had woken up screaming in the middle of the night after bad dreams and had jumped out of bed and run to Patrick's room. She had picked him up and held him tight in her arms. She had pushed her face against him, crying and shaking as she held him until slowly her crying stopped and she put him down gently in his bed. She had not returned to their bedroom and John had got up and gone to her and led her back to bed.

'What was it?' he asked as he put his arms around her and held her. 'What was it, my love, what happened?' he repeated.

'I don't know, I don't know. I just knew that something bad had happened to Patrick. I don't know what. I was looking for him; I couldn't find him anywhere. I don't know, I don't know, I don't know

9

what it was. I was just so frightened.'

He held her again as she started to cry once more and held her like that until she fell asleep. At first she moved and even shook in his arms and then she fell into a more gentle sleep, her breath soft on his cheek.

When she had woken she had not wanted to talk about the dream, had not wanted to remember and so they had let it go. But later that same day she had run from their car with Patrick in her arms as John had started the engine. Since then she had refused to go anywhere in the car. Since then, if she had to go anywhere, she went on foot, carrying Patrick in her arms. She stopped every time a car came past, her lips pressed together in a tight line, her hands held around Patrick as if to protect him, as if she was afraid something was going to happen to him.

It was strange, John thought, to feel so successful and so worried at the same time. He picked up the phone again to call Rachel, his earlier excitement now gone, and he wondered what it was his wife was trying to protect Patrick from.

Chapter 2
Happy birthday

'You haven't forgotten the birthday this week,' said Rachel the moment she recognised his voice on the phone.

John didn't reply immediately. It was not that he had forgotten Patrick's birthday, more that he was surprised and pleased by the sound of her voice. She sounded happy, she sounded excited. She didn't sound worried. It was her old voice, her beautiful soft voice, and it felt to him like a ghost from the past, a very welcome ghost. His shoulders relaxed, he breathed out deeply and he smiled at the phone. He almost wanted to say 'welcome back', but he didn't want to talk about the last few weeks. He was afraid this moment might change, that by talking about it the worries and fears of the last few weeks might come back. Instead he said, 'Our son's first birthday, how could I forget that? What kind of father do you think I am?' His voice was light, cheerful as he continued. 'I just wasn't sure what to do for his birthday. I mean, this is a special day, for him, for all of us, and I just wanted to do something special and...'

The idea came to him as he spoke to her. Of course, it would be perfect.

'And I have an idea. Let's go to Ireland for a little holiday. Let's go back to our place, to the little island. I can't think of a better place to spend Patrick's birthday.'

'Wow! Are you serious? Can we? Can you really get time off work? When do we go?'

He laughed at her questions. One moment she didn't believe him, the next moment she was organising it all.

'Yes. Yes. Yes, my boss loves me. At the end of the week.' John answered the questions in turn and then added, 'I'll book tickets now and I'll tell you why my boss loves me later when I get home.'

Ireland, the cliffs and the tiny island off the west coast. They had gone there for their first ever holiday together. A holiday where they had danced together at the top of the Cliffs of Moher, cliffs that stood straight out of the sea to a height of over one hundred metres. They had danced to the music he sang in her ear. Rachel was wearing a light white summer dress and he changed the words of a popular song and sang instead to his 'lady in white'.

'Ireland will be cold,' he had warned her. But he was happy to be wrong and he had held her close and felt her warm and soft against him. On that holiday they had decided to get married, and Patrick had been born less than nine months after the holiday. And so they called him Patrick, an Irish name. Yes, Ireland was a very special place for them.

'And you really can get time off work?'

'Yes, yes, yes. I told you, my boss loves me. I'm just going to have lunch with Jenny now and then I'll come home and we can plan our trip.'

'Let's hire a car when we get there and then we can drive around a bit.'

A car. It was her suggestion. She had seemed afraid of cars for the last few weeks and now she had suggested hiring one. She really was herself again, thought John, and he felt very pleased.

* * *

For lunch Jenny suggested a small Italian restaurant behind St Paul's Cathedral. They took a taxi there. They were still feeling very happy and excited about the success of their series, and they laughed and joked like teenagers all the way to the restaurant.

When they arrived, they ordered a bottle of the restaurant's best red wine. When the food came, they ate slowly, taking pleasure in the food. They did not often go out for lunch. They normally had a sandwich at work if they ate anything at all. And when they did find time to go out for lunch, they usually ate quickly and talked and talked without looking at what they were eating.

But this time the talk about work could wait until after they had finished their meal and were relaxing over coffee.

'So, what's your new idea and why can't it wait until tomorrow?' Jenny asked as she finished her rich cheesecake and looked at the plate to make sure she had not missed anything.

'It's not such a new idea. But anyway, first I have to tell you that I'm taking a week off for a little holiday. So you can work while I rest!'

She smiled at him and said, 'You rest and I work, there's certainly nothing new about that. What's the idea?'

'Do you remember some time ago we talked about those urban myths? You know, those stories that people tell in different places all over the country. It's always the same basic story, but the story is told as if it happened in that place, in that town or village. You know what I mean? And no one is sure if they are actually true or not. Do you remember?'

'Yeah, you mean like the story about the car in the middle of the forest,' she said.

'Which story is that?' John asked.

'You know, the story about the couple driving home late at night through a forest. They run out of petrol and the man goes to get some and the woman stays in the car. And she waits and waits and the man doesn't come back.' Jenny began to speak more quietly and more slowly as she got excited by her own storytelling. 'After a little while she hears a noise on the roof of the car. Like someone is knocking on the roof. And she's frightened and locks the doors and then a police car comes up behind. A policeman gets out of his car and shouts at her, "Get out of your car and walk towards me and don't look back" and...'

'Yeah, that sort of thing,' John said with a smile, but didn't let her finish. Jenny made a face as if she was disappointed not to be able to finish the story.

'That same story, and others like it are told in different towns all over Britain, as if they were true, but no one can ever find any evidence for them, no police records, no hospital records, nothing. Well, my idea is to try to collect some more of these stories and find out where they come from. I want to see if people have always told stories like this and if they have, what stories they used to tell years ago. Maybe we could make a programme out of it. I don't know. What do you think?'

Jenny was nodding thoughtfully. 'Maybe,' she said. 'It just reminded me of something I read the other day about a mysterious hitch-hiker. You know the kind of thing?'

John shook his head gently as if he was thinking of something else, as if he was already on holiday.

'Well, you know what a hitch-hiker is, don't you?' Jenny asked, jokingly.

'I should know,' said John, 'that's how I met Rachel! That's how we met.' He smiled at the memory and Jenny realised the serious talk was over and that he wanted to get home to his wife and son.

'OK, I'll see what I can find. I'll do some work while you rest.'

'That's how we met,' was the thought in John's head as he left the restaurant. Hitch-hiking. That's how Rachel and he had met.

Chapter 3
The lady in white

It was Friday morning, John's last day at work before their holiday in Ireland. John had bought plane tickets to Ireland and booked the same cottage they had stayed in before, on a small island off the west coast of Ireland. He had also booked a car at Dublin Airport. Everything was ready and he was looking forward to the holiday. He was thinking about nothing else. He wasn't thinking about work when the telephone rang.

It was Jenny.

'You're still here, then?' she asked.

'Oh yes, I'll be here for some time yet.'

'I don't suppose you want to talk about work, do you?' she asked.

'Well, to be honest, not really,' he said. 'Why? Do you have something you want to tell me?'

'Maybe.'

'Maybe?'

'Just something I thought you might be interested in,' Jenny said. 'Something I found about the urban myths we talked about the other day at lunch.'

'Really? You have been busy!'

'Well, I haven't been busy planning a holiday,' she laughed.

'OK. Thank you for that little joke. Now, what have you found?' John asked.

'Well, I telephoned different local newspapers and radio stations,' Jenny explained. 'I guessed that the local ones were more likely to cover these kinds of stories. I gave them the example stories we talked about and asked them to phone me if they had anything. I also looked through the Internet and checked the central library to see what books I could find.'

'And did you find anything?'

'A couple of interesting reports that I still want to check out and...' She paused. There was a long silence on the phone. She had obviously found something interesting and she was playing with him, making him wait. It was one of their games.

John laughed down the phone. He liked playing the game too so he waited a while before asking.

'And did you find anything interesting?'

'Yes.'

'So tell me,' John said.

'Do you have time?'

'Jenny!' he said in a louder voice that suggested he was becoming a little tired of the game.

'OK, OK. But not on the phone.'

'Why not on the phone?' he asked.

'Because I have something I want you to listen to as well.'

'OK, but come now. I really do have other things to do today. OK?'

The door of his office opened less than two minutes later and Jenny walked in.

John laughed again.

'You really don't waste time, do you?'

Jenny laughed back and put a cassette player on the desk in front of him.

'What's this?' John asked.

'I'll play it to you in a minute, but let me just tell you how I found it first, OK?' she said.

'OK.'

'Here it is. It's the hitch-hiker story I mentioned on Tuesday. I found three hitch-hiker stories from different local newspapers or radio stations in different parts of the country. I mean, really different parts of the country. One from Glasgow, one from Liverpool and one from a small village outside Cambridge. But...' and she paused again, keeping

John waiting again, '...the stories are exactly the same...*exactly* the same. Three different men in three different places all telling exactly the same story.'

'Maybe they know each other,' he said.

'I don't think so. Like I say, they live in different parts of the country. They work in quite different jobs and the stories they tell happened in different years. But, anyway, the really interesting thing is, they all say this happened to them in exactly the same place, just north of Brighton.'

'So, why did they come to Brighton?' he asked. 'I mean it's one of my favourite places for a weekend out of London, but what about them?'

'Again, different reasons. One man was on business. Another had taken his daughter back to the university there and the third...' she checked her notes, '...had been to a football match.'

'So, what *did* happen to them?'

'Well, listen for yourself,' Jenny said as she took a cassette from her jacket pocket and put it in the cassette player.

'This is from the local radio station in Liverpool. They talked to one of the men. I don't think they took it very seriously. They used it as part of a programme at Halloween. You know, all about ghost stories and things like that. But, of course, the radio station didn't know about the other two men. Anyway, they sent me this yesterday. I think you'll find it interesting.'

'Let's listen,' said John pressing the play button himself. He wanted to hear the story, but he also wanted to get away from work and start his holiday as soon as possible.

The cassette was silent for a moment and then the recording began. The interviewer spoke first.

So tell us what actually happened.

Well, I was driving back from Brighton. I had taken my daughter there, back to the university. She's twenty-two but my wife still worries a lot about her so I drive her there myself. And I was on my way back home. It's a long drive but I like driving at night. Less traffic. The weather was good. It was a clear, dry night. And I had just driven through a small village and was still going quite slowly and then, just outside the village I saw a woman. She was standing at the side of the road and...all dressed in white she was, so I saw her immediately. And as I drove past she put her hand out as if she was hitch-hiking and I stopped. I mean, I don't normally stop for hitch-hikers because, well you never know who you're going to pick up, do you? But, a woman, late at night, and I

thought of my daughter and I know how I would feel if she was out by herself late at night, so I stopped.

And then?

She walked up behind the car. I opened the door and asked her where she was going. 'The nearest garage, please,' she said. So I said, 'Get in.' She said, 'Thank you.' She got in and I drove on. I saw that she hadn't put on her seat belt. I mentioned this to her and she looked at me and then started crying. She didn't say anything at all; she just started crying. She didn't say a word; she just started crying. I didn't know what was going on. I asked her, 'Are you all right?' but she obviously wasn't and she didn't answer and she just kept on crying. I didn't know what to do. I didn't know what to say. I just drove on. I didn't know if I should stop or...or, do something else. I just didn't know. And I had just about decided to stop the car when she said, 'I'm sorry I...' and she was still breathing really fast, as if she was fighting to breathe. But she had stopped crying. I still felt like my stomach was in my mouth and my hair was standing on end...I didn't know what to do.

And then she said, 'I'm sorry, I'm sorry. We had a bit of a problem with the car. That's why I'm going to the garage. The others are waiting at the car. I don't know why I started crying like that. I'm sorry.'

I asked if I could help with the car. I asked her where the car was and she said, 'No, thank you. The garage will be able to help.' And she said the car was just outside the village where I had stopped for her. Well, I didn't remember seeing any other car parked on the road outside the village, but I didn't want to disagree with her, you know. I didn't want her to start crying again. She was quiet again and then I noticed she was shaking. 'Are you cold? I can put the heater on.' She thanked me and said it was because of the rain and how she was still wet. I turned to look at her for a moment and noticed her face was wet, and her hair, and her dress. 'Was it raining here?' I asked. Because I had not seen a drop of rain that day, anywhere.

John put his hand on the cassette player and pressed a button. The tape stopped.

'He hasn't finished yet,' Jenny said.

'Where did you get this?' John's voice was strange, very cold.

Jenny looked at him. He had a strange look on his face. Jenny had never seen John like this, had never heard his voice like this. She felt suddenly cold all down her back. His voice and his look made her feel uncomfortable. They made her feel more frightened than the story on the cassette had.

'I told you, from Liverpool. From the local radio station there.'

John was staring at the cassette player. He was very still and his face had gone completely white.

'What's the matter, John? Are you OK? John?'

He didn't seem to hear her and continued to sit still for a few moments and then he looked up at her.

'What's going on here? Is this some kind of a joke? Is this your joke?'

'No. What do you mean, joke? What are you talking about? John, what are you talking about? There's no joke. John, you're frightening me. What do you mean?'

He looked at her for a minute, not speaking, just staring at her, as if he was trying to see inside her, to see what she was thinking. Then he nodded his head slowly as if to show he believed that she was not playing a joke on him.

'Maybe he knows me.'

'Who? Maybe who knows you?'

He looked towards the cassette player. 'Him. The man telling this story. But, why would he do this?'

'Do what? What are you talking about, John?' she asked, worried. This was not a joke, not her joke and clearly it was not a joke for him either.

'This is *my* story,' he said so softly she hardly heard him, and then he repeated it a little louder. 'This is *my story.*'

'Your story? But how? I told you, John. There were three men. They all told the same story. How could it be your story?'

Again John was silent, sitting and staring at the desk. It was impossible to know what was going on in his head. He was shaking his head from side to side now as if he was trying hard to understand something.

'What's going on here? I don't understand this. This is my story. How did he know this? How? I don't understand.'

They sat for some time on opposite sides of the desk without speaking. Jenny sat looking at John. She was worried. She was also a little frightened. She didn't know what to do. Should she get help? Leave him? Stay with him? Say something? Get him a drink? What should she do? What could she do...?

Chapter 4
Losing control

Jenny was still trying to decide what to do when John suddenly moved his hand out towards the cassette player and pressed the play button again. The voice on the cassette continued telling the story.

...And she said it had been raining all day and maybe that was why they had the problem with the car. And then she went quiet and I was afraid she might start crying again so I didn't say anything more. I didn't ask any more questions. I just drove. And it was a lovely night, I couldn't understand how it could have been raining here because the road was as dry as...I don't know what, but it was just very dry.

And then, after a while, I felt that she was looking at me again. I tried not to notice. I didn't want to look back at her. I mean she was really beautiful. I noticed that the minute she got into the car. Really beautiful. Dark hair and clear blue eyes. I could see them when I opened the door and the light came on inside the car. Really lovely. And normally I would have been very happy to look at her, and for her to look at me.

But there was something very strange about this whole situation and it was beginning to make me feel nervous.

And I was beginning to wonder why she was crying about a car. I mean I know it's a problem when something goes wrong with your car, especially at night, but it is only a machine, isn't it? And you can get it repaired and...and there must be a garage somewhere around here. So I was thinking, 'Why is she crying about this?' And then I thought, 'Maybe it's not the car, maybe something else has happened, maybe she was with a man or something and he...and he did something...' And so I was about to ask her...if she really was all right and I turned to look at her and she was looking at me.

She was looking at me...it's difficult to describe the look but...I don't know what it was, it was like she was trying to see what kind of person I was. It was, I don't know, it was almost sexy and yet uncertain, as if she didn't know if she could trust me or not. I mean, after the tears and everything, it made me feel sort of excited and nervous at the same time. And a bit uncomfortable. I mean, she was not much older than my daughter.

Anyway, I didn't like her looking at me like that,

29

and I looked away, back to the road. When I saw the sign that said there was a garage in five hundred metres, I felt almost happy. I just wanted to get her out of the car. I said, 'We'll soon be there,' but she didn't answer. Then suddenly, as I was getting close to a bend in the road, she started to scream. I went cold inside and my stomach jumped and she was screaming, 'Oh God, we're losing control, we're losing control. Watch out, watch out, oh my God!'

And I was just staring at the road, and...nothing. There was nothing there. The road was empty. The car was going the same as before. There was nothing. Nothing was happening. So I turned to look at her, and as I did, she suddenly put her hands on the steering wheel of the car and pulled it...

John had been sitting listening quietly to the story without moving, but now he suddenly changed his position in his chair. He shook his head a few times, as if he was disagreeing with someone.

'No, it wasn't like that. No, it wasn't like that. No, she didn't do that, no.'

Jenny sat staring at him. What was John talking about? What did he mean? She watched as he moved closer to the cassette player, as if to listen more carefully, although the man continued to speak in the same way, not louder, not quieter. And then the man's voice suddenly did rise and he almost shouted as he relived the memory.

...I shouted at her, 'Stop it, stop it! What are you doing? Do you want to kill us?' The car was moving from side to side as she pulled on the steering wheel and I tried to keep the car straight on the road. She was strong. She was really strong. I couldn't believe it. She wasn't big and she was quite slim. I don't know where she got the strength from. It was really difficult. I pulled the steering wheel as hard as I could with my right hand and hit her arm with my left hand.

There was a pause in the recording as if the man was embarrassed at the memory of hitting a woman, a young woman. A young woman like his own daughter, perhaps.

And then?

The car was still going from side to side. I put my foot on the brake, really hard. But with her still pulling on the wheel and me standing on the brakes like that, the car just turned round. I lost control. I really did lose control. I tried to control the car again but I couldn't. The car hit the grass at the side of the road, and jumped in the air and hit the grass again and then came to a stop. I just sat there, staring at the road, not moving. My hands were still on the steering wheel, holding it really tightly. And then, then I just blew out all the air that was inside me. It was as if I had been holding my breath all this time and my heart was going like a train. I could hear it. I could hear my heart beating as if the noise was coming from outside my body. And my hands were completely wet on the steering wheel, and I just sat there and then...and then I remembered her.

'What was that all about?' I shouted at her. 'Why did you do that? What's the matter with you?' But she just sat there, looking straight in front of her with her hand over her mouth. And then she pushed the hair from her face and I saw something on her face. Something dark was running down her face from her hair. I think it was blood. So I felt bad about shouting at her. I asked her how she was, but I think my voice was still loud. She looked at me. She looked so frightened. And then she looked away from me and she tried to open the door. At first she couldn't find the handle, but then she did find it and she managed to open the door.

She was out of the car and running back down the road before I had a chance to say anything more. I shouted something. I don't know what. I don't know what I shouted and then I tried to open my door but my seat belt was stuck—I couldn't take it off at first—and then I did get it off. I opened the door and jumped out of the car and I ran after her. I got round the bend in the road and kept running and...and then...then I just stopped. She had gone. Disappeared. There was nothing. Nobody. Just a straight, empty road. And I mean, she was wearing white, you know. It was a perfectly clear night. But I couldn't see her. She wasn't there. And there were no other roads, no turnings. There was nothing at the side of the road, just an open field, on both sides of the road. It just wasn't possible for her to disappear. I just stood there, looking all around me and then a car came racing towards me along the road. Its lights almost blinded me and the driver blew his horn as he drove past. He probably thought I was drunk. I felt as if I was drunk. I felt very strange.

I walked back to the car and sat there for a while, staring at nothing. But then two more cars came round the corner and blew their horns at me. Then I realised my car was facing the wrong direction and I kind of woke up. I decided to drive back and see what I could find. I drove as far as the village where I had picked her up, but there was nothing. No lady in white, no cars parked at the side of the road with people waiting in them. *Nothing. I didn't know what to do. Report it to the police? Report what? That I gave a young woman a lift in the car, that she cried, that she went mad and almost caused an accident? That she disappeared into thin air? I couldn't! I couldn't...*

But I couldn't drive on either, and it was too late to find a hotel or anything like that. I decided to stop and try to get some sleep in the car and then drive on. But I didn't want to stop near that village. I don't know why, but I was afraid. I didn't know what to think, but I was sure I didn't want to see that woman again.

It was Jenny who turned the cassette player off. She had heard it before and knew the man had finished his story.

There was silence in the room. As the man had told his story, Jenny had not taken her eyes off John. As the man had talked about the accident, John had continued to shake his head, and whispered 'No, no' a couple more times. Now he just sat there, not moving, not saying anything, just staring at the cassette player. Jenny was feeling very uncomfortable. While the man had been telling his story on the cassette she had not felt so bad, but now that the voice on the cassette had stopped, now that there was just John and her in the room, she felt very alone. She wanted to ask him to explain but she was afraid. She had never seen him like this. He sat there in his own world and she was afraid to ask him any more questions.

They continued to sit there for some time and then John took a deep, deep breath, then another, and then he looked up at her. His face was very calm now.

'Get your car keys,' he said quietly. 'I'll drive. And bring your mobile phone, we'll need it, and the telephone numbers of those three men. Have you got them?'

She nodded and was pleased that she had the telephone numbers, pleased that she did not have to speak. She did not know if she could control her voice.

'Come on,' he said and got up and walked quickly towards the door.

She didn't ask him where they were going. She was still not sure about her voice. She also had a feeling that she already knew where they were going, but she couldn't quite believe it.

Chapter 5
A journey into the past

They drove across Waterloo Bridge and down the busy main road to the large roundabout at Elephant and Castle, that strangely named part of London south of the river. There was no elephant and no castle, just a lot of dirty, grey office buildings with a large shopping centre in the middle of a very large roundabout.

It was at the roundabout that Jenny saw a road sign for Brighton. 'So, we are going there,' she thought. 'We are going to the village where these men met the hitch-hiker.'

She looked at John, but he said nothing. He continued to look straight ahead.

They drove on. Jenny looked out the window. No tourists ever came to this part of the city. There was nothing of interest here, only large areas of houses and flats. Every few kilometres there was a little group of shops in streets that were always called High Street. The streets all looked the same. The shops too were always the same: Boots, W. H. Smith,

Woolworths. You could be in any part of London or in any town in Britain and find exactly the same shops.

There was nothing of interest here for Jenny either but she looked at everything she passed as if she had never been here in her life. It was better to watch everything they passed than to think of what they were doing, to think of where they were going. It was better to do this than try to guess what was going on in John's mind.

She had worked with John for over three years. They knew each other very well. She had often thought she knew what John was thinking. She could sometimes finish his sentences for him. But now, she had no idea what he was thinking. She was not sure if she wanted to know what he was thinking.

He drove in complete silence, not even saying a word as the driver of another car pulled out suddenly in front of them and John had to brake quickly. This reminded Jenny to put on her seat belt and, as she put it on, she thought of the story on the cassette. The man had said something about a seat belt in the story. She tried to remember exactly what he had said, but the only thing that came to her mind was the question she had been asking herself since they left the office.

What did John mean when he said 'this is my story'? What was in this story that had made her boss turn white and go silent? She had never known John to remain silent for so long. He normally talked a lot and was quiet only when he was trying to understand something. He still looked at her at those times, even if he said nothing. But now his face showed nothing. He stared straight in front of the car. Jenny returned her attention to what was outside the car.

They were on the road that took them around Croydon, to the south of London. They drove past the old airport that had once been London's main airport. This was where the British prime minister, Neville Chamberlain, had returned to after a meeting with Hitler before the 1939–1945 war. He had waved a piece of paper as he climbed down from the plane. A piece of paper that Hitler had signed. 'Peace in our time' is what Chamberlain had said of this agreement he had signed with Hitler. Jenny could see the picture in her head, although all of this had happened long before she was born. Even her father had only been a child when all this had happened. It was a story Jenny knew from other people, but it was not her story, it did not touch her in any direct way. It was not *her* story.

'This is *my* story,' John had said.

She could not get the sentence out of her head. She could still hear John's voice as he had said this and the disbelief on his face. She could not get this out of her head. What did he mean?

Journalists sometimes said 'this is my story' when they were writing about something and they did not want other journalists to write about it. But John had not meant that. He and Jenny worked together on stories. There was no competition between them. So what did he mean?

They were leaving the city behind them as they travelled south. They left the rows of small houses with living rooms that were only a few metres away from the speeding traffic, houses with no gardens for children to play in. It wasn't a safe place for children with all this traffic. Now the houses were big with big gardens. Then they were in the open countryside, with less traffic and more signs for Brighton. They were getting close.

Just before they joined the motorway, she noticed a car parked at the side of the road and a man standing looking at it. She watched him in the side mirror as they drove past without slowing down. He was standing looking at the engine. He was well dressed and she guessed he did not know much about engines. She smiled as she thought of herself in similar situations. She also knew nothing about cars. She remembered being with a boyfriend once in his car. They had gone for a walk in a forest park. A beautiful place, she remembered. But when they got back to the car and tried to start the engine, nothing happened. Her boyfriend had looked at the engine and, although he found the problem quickly, he had not been able to repair it himself.

'I have an idea,' he had said to her, 'you stay here and look at the engine helplessly, I'll go over to that café. I need the toilet anyway.'

Jenny had wondered what he was talking about. But within two minutes another man had appeared from nowhere and had offered to help her, and had repaired the car. She smiled again at the memory. She had not seen much of that boyfriend after that and she had always bought the best cars she could afford for herself. She didn't want to break down in the middle of the night somewhere, in the middle of nowhere. Not like that lady in white, hitch-hiking on a lonely road at night.

The smile disappeared from Jenny's face as she remembered something else now, something John had said in that Italian restaurant. Something about Rachel. Something he had said when they were talking about hitch-hiking. Yes, now she remembered his words. He had said, 'That's how Rachel and I met. Hitch-hiking. That's how we met.'

Jenny suddenly felt cold inside. 'That's my story.' John's words came back to her again and slowly a new question entered Jenny's mind. Was it possible that John had met Rachel in the same way that the man on the cassette had described?

'That's not possible.'

She realised that she had said these words out loud and had not thought them silently. She turned nervously towards John, but he continued to stare ahead as if he had heard nothing. She was happy he had not heard. She did not want to tell him what she was thinking. She was not sure herself what she was thinking. The same phrase continued in her head, repeated again and again. 'That's not possible. That's not possible.'

What had she thought as she had listened to the voice on the cassette and heard the stories from the other two men? That this was an interesting example of how the same story can travel from place to place, all over the country, and be retold in exactly the same way, as if it was true, as if it really happened? Had she for a moment thought that there was some truth in the story itself? What truth? That this woman was a ghost?

'That's not possible.'

Again she was not sure if she had spoken out loud or just thought this, or if indeed John had spoken these words. She turned and looked at him. He was shaking his head slowly from side to side, as if he was also thinking, 'That's not possible.' Had John actually spoken these words? Was John thinking the same thoughts as her?

But she had no time to think any more about it. At the side of the road she saw the name of the next village. She recognised the name of the village from the men's story. They were arriving in the village where the three men had met the hitch-hiker.

She sat completely still as John drove into the village. He continued to drive without slowing down and a new thought came to her suddenly. The man on the cassette had not mentioned the name of the village! *She* knew it from what the reporters from the local radio stations had told her. The man on the cassette had not mentioned the name, and she had not told John.

'So maybe we are not going to stop here,' she thought. 'Maybe we are going somewhere else. Maybe this is not the same as John's story.' As these thoughts filled her head, John looked in the car's rear-view mirror, slowed down and turned the car round. He drove back through the village and stopped just outside it on the other side of the road from where Jenny had seen the name of the village.

And then John spoke to her, for the first time since they had left the office. His voice was quiet and calm.

'This is where I first met Rachel. This is where I first met my wife. She was hitch-hiking. She was standing right there. I was driving back to London. I stopped my car. She was standing right there. I gave her a lift. She was wearing a dress. She was wearing a white dress. She was standing right there...'

Chapter 6

The policeman's story—the accident

Jenny was speaking on her mobile telephone. She was standing a couple of metres away from John, who watched and listened as she spoke. It was his idea to phone one of the three men who had met the hitch-hiker. That is why he had told her to bring the phone and the telephone numbers as they left the office. She was talking to one of the men. She had tried another number already but there was no answer. With the second number the phone was answered almost immediately and the man was pleased to hear from her.

John could only hear Jenny's part of the conversation.

'Yes, we're just outside the village.'

'Yes, going north towards London.'

Jenny turned round to look at something behind her.

'Yes, I can see that.'

'Yes.'

'OK, thank you for your help.'

'Yes, I'll phone you if we decide to make the programme.'

'Thank you. Yes, goodbye. No, I don't think that will be necessary. Goodbye.'

Jenny put the phone back in her jacket pocket.

She and John stood looking at each other for a moment. 'So this is the place where he met the hitch-hiker?' John asked.

'Yeah. This is the place.'

'He's sure?' John asked.

'He said he would never forget this place. Yes, it's the same place,' Jenny replied.

'And the same place where I met Rachel.'

Jenny did not know what to say. What did this all mean? What did it mean that Rachel and John had met at the same place where the three men had met the mysterious hitch-hiker?

They continued to look at each other without speaking. Neither of them knew what to say and neither of them seemed to know what to do now. Finally Jenny broke the silence.

'I'm going to phone the police,' she said.

'Why?'

Jenny didn't answer John. She didn't know herself why she was phoning the police. She just knew she had to do something. She didn't want to stand there alone with John in the silence of his unspoken thoughts and her own unspoken thoughts. When she felt uncomfortable in a situation, Jenny always had to do something. She hated uncomfortable silences. It always made her feel better to move, to do something. Usually what she did was to run away as fast as she could. She had left many boyfriends like that. But, although she felt uncomfortable here, this was her work—she could not leave John alone.

She phoned the operator and got the number of the police station in Brighton. The police in Brighton suggested she talked to the local police in a village a few kilometres away. They told her how to get there.

* * *

It took them a long time to find the police station, although the village was not large. The police station was an ordinary-looking house, a house in its own garden. A car stood outside. It was a blue car, very clean with nothing lying around inside, no cassettes, no magazines, no waste paper. It didn't look like a family car but it also didn't look like the normal white police cars with their bright red and blue markings. The word 'Police' was written in quite small letters on the side of the car and nowhere else. The Police sign on the wall just beside the front door was also small.

It was difficult to believe that it really was a police station at all. But when the door opened there was a policeman in his dark blue uniform standing there. He was a middle-aged man, probably in his late fifties. He smiled at them. Jenny imagined that not many people came to see him—it didn't look like a busy police station. The policeman invited them into a small office and then into the living room beside it.

'We'll be more comfortable in here,' he said.

Jenny was not surprised when the policeman offered a cup of tea before they could explain why they were there. Jenny accepted. She was doing all the talking and John sat down without saying anything. This was not the normal John, the John who liked to lead, who liked to take control. Jenny again remembered words from the story on the cassette. 'We're losing control. We're losing control.' She wondered for a moment if John was also losing control. She had never seen him like this. She had never seen him so quiet, not speaking, hardly moving.

While the policeman was out in the kitchen, Jenny looked around his room. It was also very tidy. It was the room of a man who had lived alone for many years. There were only a few personal things and nothing looked out of place. There was a bookcase in the corner where all the books stood in perfect order. There were no books lying on their sides, no spaces between the books, they were all standing up straight. For a moment Jenny wondered if they were real books at all, but she didn't check.

She looked instead at the three photographs on the small table beside the television. They were all black-and-white photographs. Two showed young couples, different couples, both staring back at the photographer and smiling. In one photo the couple were formally dressed and it looked as if it had been taken by a professional photographer. From their clothes it looked as if it had been taken in the 1930s.

The photograph of the second couple was taken much later, Jenny thought, and was more relaxed. On holiday somewhere, a couple with the sea behind them. The third photo showed a very young boy, perhaps only one year old. Jenny looked at the photographs and tried to imagine the relationships with the policeman. Were the older couple his parents? Were the other couple the policeman himself with his wife? Where was she now? Was the boy the policeman's son? There were no other photographs.

She wondered if his story was happy or not. She hoped it was happy. She looked at John as the policeman brought the tea. John, she thought, was looking at the picture of the young boy. The boy was probably about the same age as Patrick, she thought. Yes, she hoped this would be a happy story.

* * *

The policeman looked thoughtful as Jenny explained why they had come and told him the story of the mysterious hitch-hiker.

'Have you heard any stories like that around?' Jenny asked him.

The policeman smiled.

'Well, I can't say that I have. It's very quiet round here, not a lot happens, so if something does happen, everyone talks about it, you know what I mean,' and he laughed quietly. 'This is a quiet place. If anything happens people love to talk about it, to gossip. So I'm sure I would have heard any ghost stories.'

Jenny thought he looked quickly at the photograph of the young couple near the sea, but she was more interested in what he had said. 'Ghost.' The word that neither she nor John had spoken. The word that she had not wanted to think and certainly not to say, not since John had listened to the story on the cassette. Not since John had said, 'this is my story.'

The policeman continued talking as John looked towards Jenny.

'You say they met this woman near the village? All three of the men met her in the same place?'

'Four.'

The policeman looked at John and John repeated, 'Four. Four men met her.'

'I'm sorry, I thought you said three men had reported this incident,' said the policeman as he looked again at Jenny. For the first time he sounded almost formal, more like a normal policeman.

'Maybe four,' said Jenny and then quickly continued.

'But, yes, in the same place, just north of the village, near the sign for the village actually.'

'Near that sign, you say?' He thought for a while, his face showing the effort he was making as he tried to remember. Then his wide smile appeared again— he had remembered.

'Yes, there was something, of course there was, I'd forgotten.'

He had been looking up at the ceiling as he tried to remember. Now, as his eyes came down and he looked at Jenny, the smile disappeared completely.

'It was an accident,' he said and he looked down at the floor. 'A terrible accident.' He looked as if he would rather not say anything more about it, as if remembering the accident had brought back feelings that were very painful.

He got up and went out to his office and when he returned after a few minutes he was carrying some papers. He sat down and started to speak, not touching the papers that lay on his knees.

'It was what we call an SCA.' And again his voice was more formal. 'That's what we call it, an SCA. A Single Car Accident. Just one car. Then happen. Sometimes the driver is drunk. Sometimes it might even be someone trying to kill themselves. Suicide.'

He looked up at Jenny as he said this and then added quickly, 'I'm sorry, Miss, I didn't mean to suggest that happened in this case. I'm sure this had nothing to do with drink or...or with suicide. It's just that sometimes...'

He didn't finish the sentence. He seemed worried about Jenny. It was as if he was talking to the family of someone who had been in a road accident and not to television journalists. Jenny nodded her head and smiled at the policeman. She normally didn't like people calling her 'Miss'. She certainly did not like people behaving differently towards her because she was a woman. But she couldn't get angry with this friendly policeman who looked so unhappy himself at the memory of this accident.

'Go on,' she whispered.

'The driver seemed to lose control coming around

the bend out of the village. Maybe she was going too fast. Maybe something happened inside the car. We don't know. We checked the car afterwards and couldn't find anything wrong with the brakes or the steering wheel. It's difficult to tell though, after that kind of accident.'

He looked at them.

'Do you really want to know more about this?' he asked.

Jenny nodded. The policeman continued.

'It had been a very rainy night.'

John sat forward in his chair as the policeman said this. It was the first time he had moved since he had sat down in the policeman's living room, the first time he had shown that he was listening, that he was interested.

'Very wet,' the policeman continued, 'and the car left the road and hit a tree and that was it. They...they were both killed immediately.'

'They?' John and Jenny asked together.

'The woman...and...and the child. People from the village heard the crash and ran out. There was a doctor who lived nearby but...but there was nothing he could do. Nothing. They were both dead.'

'How old was the boy?' asked John looking at the photograph on the policeman's table.

The policeman looked surprised by the question.

'I didn't say it was a boy. How did you know that?'

John didn't say anything, but Jenny felt her heart sink as the policeman answered John's question.

'Just a baby. He wasn't even one year old.'

'Just like my son Patrick,' said John, 'just like Patrick.'

Chapter 7
John's story

The policeman continued to speak. He did not look at the papers on his knees but stared into space as if this helped him remember. He spoke calmly and without pausing.

'We tried to get in touch with her family, but we couldn't find anyone. There was an address in London on her driving licence. The police in London went to the house. They talked to neighbours. They said she had only lived there for a few months. Lived alone. I mean, she and the baby lived alone. They said she was very quiet, but she didn't go out much.

'She was always friendly when she met the neighbours outside, but she didn't talk much about herself. She obviously loved the baby. She seemed happy. The neighbours hadn't noticed any visitors coming to the house. They were surprised that there was no man around. You know how people are. They see a woman with a young baby and they wonder why there's no man around. But anyway, they hadn't seen any man or any other visitors, except the week before the accident.

'The neighbours said a young woman had come to stay about a week earlier. They looked very like each other, the two women. The neighbours thought that maybe they were sisters. The other woman looked as if she had come from a hot country, they said. She was very brown, very suntanned. And the police found a half-packed suitcase in the flat. They didn't know whose case it was. There was no address on it, nothing. They couldn't even tell if it was half packed or half unpacked, if someone had just arrived or if someone was planning to leave.

They checked the Registry Office in London, and found dates of birth for the woman and a sister. They also found records of their parents' deaths. But that was all they found. The Tax Office had records for the woman but not the sister. The records showed she had worked for a computer company for two years, but then left. The company didn't know any more about her. And that was it. That's all we ever found out. A single car accident. A woman and baby killed. No family found. Sad. Very sad.'

There was a long silence now. The policeman looked at the floor as he finished his story. Then he turned and looked again towards the photographs. As he moved in his chair, the papers fell from his knees and the noise seemed to wake him from his thoughts. He bent down to pick them up. He stopped as something on one of the pages caught his eye. He nodded his head and spoke softly, almost to himself.

'Of course, the other woman.'

He looked up at them, still nodding his head as he remembered.

'There was something else. Something a bit strange. Some of the villagers remembered seeing a young woman by the car. She was a stranger. I mean they didn't know her, she wasn't from the village. She was standing a few metres away from the car. She wasn't looking at the car, she was just standing, holding her handbag close to her chest and she was crying. One of the villagers put an arm round her, trying to make her feel better. He didn't know if she had been in the car or not. Or maybe from another car that had seen the accident and had stopped.'

The policeman paused, trying to remember more and then when he couldn't, he looked through the papers for a minute. He seemed disappointed that his memory had failed him. Then he continued.

'The ambulance arrived soon after and the villager went to help. He told the ambulance people about the other woman. He thought that maybe they should look at her and make sure that she was all right. But they couldn't find her. They looked for her but they couldn't find her.'

He looked again at the papers and read aloud: 'A young woman, dressed in white, was also seen near the scene of the accident but she left before any police officer was able to talk to her.'

* * *

Jenny drove away from the police station with John sitting in the passenger seat. They drove back to the village where the accident had happened. They drove past the place where they had stopped earlier. The place where John had given Rachel a lift. Neither of them spoke. They drove on and, after a few minutes, came to a petrol station.

'Stop here,' John said.

Jenny parked the car behind the petrol station. Even before the car had stopped, John had started speaking, and speaking very quickly.

'This is where I dropped Rachel that night. I dropped her here and this is different from the other men's stories. This is different. I gave her a lift and she was wet and she was wearing a white dress. We had the same conversation about the car, the same as the man on the cassette said. She did start crying. All that was the same. She did look at me the way that man on the cassette described. But I looked back at her and we smiled. We smiled at each other and then we came here and I stopped.'

So, this is what John had meant by 'This is my story', Jenny thought. In a way she was not surprised by what he had just told her.

'She didn't shout anything? She didn't put her hands on the steering wheel?'

'No, no. Nothing like that. I left her here. I asked her again if she was sure I couldn't help. She said "no", she said "thank you", she smiled, she got out of the car. But she didn't close the door immediately. She seemed to be waiting for something. And I just asked her if, maybe, I could see her again. I said I would like to phone her some time to make sure...'

John smiled at the memory. This was the first smile Jenny had seen from him for a long time and she reached out her hand and touched him on the arm.

'I wanted to see her again,' John said.

'And you did, you did see her again and...' Jenny stopped. She had no idea how to continue.

John put his hands up to his face. Jenny was not sure if he was crying or not, but when he spoke again, his voice was breaking.

'What the hell is this all about, Jenny? What does all this have to do with me, with Rachel? What does this all mean? I don't understand what's going on here. This is crazy. I don't believe this. I don't...I don't know what to believe.'

'What do you want it to mean, for God's sake?' Jenny was almost shouting at him now. She was not angry with him, but shouting at him like this gave her more confidence in what she was saying.

'You met Rachel on the road. She said she had a problem with her car. You gave her a lift to the petrol station. You thought she was beautiful. She *is* beautiful. You wanted to see her again. You asked her out. You did see her again. You fell in love. You...you know what happened after that. What else do you want to think? Why do you want to think anything else?'

'And these other men's stories?' he asked.

'Their story is similar to yours, yes, but there are differences. You said that yourself. There are differences. I know it's unusual. It's strange, but that's all it is. Something very unusual, but it doesn't mean anything. Their stories have nothing to do with you.'

'And what about their stories?' John asked. 'What do you think happened to them? Who do you think their lady in white was? What does your journalist's mind have to say about that?'

Jenny paused, but only for a moment. She liked being a journalist.

'The woman. You know, the woman at the accident. That could have been the sister. The sister of the woman in the car. Maybe she was in the car too. Maybe she lost her memory because of the accident. It happens to people in accidents. They don't know where they are or who they are. Sometimes they lose their memory for a long time. So this woman is in shock. She walks off into the night. I don't know where to, and she doesn't know where she is going either. She just walks off, somewhere. Maybe someone gave her a lift. Maybe someone found her and helped her, but she couldn't remember anything. Later, she remembers this place. She doesn't remember anything else but she does remember this place, so she comes back here. She hopes she will remember everything. It happens. People in accidents hit their heads. They lose their memories. No one is looking for her. Her only relative is killed in the accident, so no one reports her missing. It happens.'

Jenny's voice was getting excited now, caught up by her own storytelling again.

'Anyway, she comes back, she comes back to this place. She remembers it, she remembers getting a lift from somewhere near here. She wants to remember the rest. That's why she comes back here. She doesn't know who she is or what she has lost. She doesn't know what has happened to her. She doesn't know anything. It's not just her memory she's looking for. There could be people out there waiting for her, looking for her, she doesn't know. She hopes that maybe coming back here and getting another lift will help her remember. So she tries. She tries again and again and again.'

'Until she meets me?'

'Will you get this out of your head? We are not talking about Rachel!' Jenny was almost screaming at John now. 'This is a *different* person. The fact that you met Rachel here is just a coincidence! Cars do break down, you know, and women do get wet in the rain, and you know perfectly well that it can be raining here and completely dry down the road. This is England, not the Sahara Desert!'

She was angry with him now, but she wasn't sure why. Maybe it was because she was frightened, frightened that John wouldn't believe her, frightened because she didn't know if she believed it herself.

'And the lady in white always disappears?'

'She does not disappear, John! She runs away from an accident she has almost caused. She is frightened, she doesn't remember her past. All she remembers is that she is coming here again and again and the same thing is happening, as if it was out of her control. And she is frightened and she runs away, and hides in a field or somewhere, anywhere. She does not want to explain to the driver what this is all about.'

Jenny sat back in the seat of the car, exhausted by her own storytelling. And yet, she thought, her story could be true. She wanted to believe that. The thought that her story was true was calming her. And it was calming John. He sat beside her, nodding his head.

'What else do you want to believe?' Jenny continued, facing her own unbelievable and unspoken fears. 'That Rachel is a ghost? Go home, put your arms round her...and Patrick. If Rachel is a ghost, what does that make Patrick? That's madness, John, that's madness. Go home, hold her in your arms and then phone me and tell me she's a ghost. OK?'

She laughed, although it was not a very natural laugh. She looked at John and she thought, she hoped, that she saw the beginning of a small smile appear in John's eyes.

'Go home to your family. Go on your holiday to Ireland. Get away from work. Get away from this story. You've been working too hard, for too long without a holiday. Go away and don't come back until you've forgotten all this.'

Chapter 8
Ireland–peace and memories

The boat left the small Irish fishing port and turned into the open Atlantic Ocean towards the island of Inishbofin. The weather was beautiful, a warm sunny day with almost no wind. The sea rose gently and slowly as if it were taking long slow breaths. Rachel stood at the back of the boat with Patrick in her arms. Patrick stared at the birds that followed the boat, sometimes flying so close to the boat that Patrick could almost touch them, smiling, happy, excited by his birthday present. John hoped the holiday would be a wonderful present for all of them.

This was only their second day in Ireland, only three days since his trip to Brighton with Jenny. John was trying to forget the journey to Brighton, and trying to forget the stories of the man on the cassette and of the policeman. He had not told Rachel about any of that last day at work. The stories had frightened him. It had frightened him that the man's story was so similar to his own first meeting with

Rachel. He didn't want to talk to Rachel about it. He would not know how to tell her or what to tell her. Anyway, talking to her would make it all seem real. He preferred to think of it as a dream, a dream that he could forget.

He hoped that being in Ireland would make him feel better, would help him forget. This was a place where he had spent many holidays by himself and where he and Rachel had spent their first holiday together. He always felt peaceful here. He hoped that those feelings of peace would come back to him now. Now more than ever he needed to have those feelings of peace.

He stood at the front of the boat and watched the seven dark round mountains of Connemara that rose behind the fishing port they had just left. They were not large mountains, not by world standards, but from the sea they looked high enough. They also looked very attractive, very inviting, very safe. But if the weather changed, and it changed very quickly here, and if the fog and rain came in from the Atlantic, then it became very dangerous. Then, when you could not see your foot in front of you in the thick fog, it became very dangerous. Then you could get lost. Then you could disappear forever.

The boat was turning now beside the Cliffs of Moher, the black cliffs that rose straight out of the sea to a height of over one hundred metres. John looked up at the cliffs, and felt small. It was difficult to believe that the tiny shapes he could just see at the top were people. They were so small, so far away.

Rachel and he had walked along these cliffs on their first holiday here. They had walked alone at sunset and had danced to the songs he sang in her ears. Then they had walked a little further until they stopped and stood silently. Both were quiet in their own thoughts before a small monument that was placed at the edge of the cliff. They bent down to read what was written on it:

To Sean

We miss you each and every day.

We live for the day when we will all meet again in a better place.

There was no date on the monument. There was nothing to show how or when Sean had died. There was nothing to show how old he was, or who had left this stone here in his memory, a metre from the edge of the cliff.

John moved closer to the edge to look down into the dark blue-green water that broke into waves far below but Rachel pulled him back sharply by his arm.

'John, don't. Be careful.'

He smiled at her.

'It's OK.'

He then bent down, picked up a small stone and threw it gently over the edge. He tried to follow its fall to the sea but he lost it long before it reached the water and he heard no sound as it hit the water and disappeared for ever into the ocean.

Shouts from people around him on the boat woke John from his memories. He looked around, not sure what was happening. Everyone was shouting. He looked for Rachel and Patrick but they were not standing where they had been. A sudden feeling of sickness rose from his stomach to the back of his mouth as he stared into the sea behind the boat.

He thought he could see something in the water. But the shouts were coming from the side of the boat and, as he ran down the steps, he could see almost everyone on the boat was there. He saw Rachel and Patrick near the side of the boat. Patrick was pointing at something and shouting. His eyes and mouth were wide open. John looked over the side of the boat but could see nothing.

But then, suddenly, something black and grey jumped out of the water and dived in again, and jumped and dived again and then again and he realised it was a dolphin and that the dolphin was swimming beside the boat, racing it.

Another dolphin appeared and the two dolphins now jumped together from the water and then dived back into the cold sea.

'Look Patrick,' he heard Rachel say as he moved behind her, 'the dolphin's mummy has come to make sure he's all right. She looks after him, just like I look after you. See?'

The smaller dolphin swam with them a little longer but the bigger one did not come back and then the small one too swam away from the side of the boat, doing a final jump as if to say goodbye.

'Good sign that,' said a man standing beside John. John was not sure who the man was talking to. 'They look after people at sea, people in danger. A sign of life too, you know, of life even after death,' the man said.

'Really?' asked John, but Patrick was shouting in his ear now about the 'fish' and John had to turn away from the man and listen to Patrick.

He saw the man again when the boat arrived at the island of Inishbofin, but only in the distance as he walked away from the port. John and Rachel waited until everyone else had got off. Then they collected all their bags, full of food and clothes, and got off the boat themselves. By that time the man had already disappeared and they did not see him again as they walked towards the cottage.

The cottage was on the east coast of the island. This was where most of the islanders lived. There were still only ten or twelve cottages here, all looking back towards the mainland of Ireland. There were also two pubs where people went for the nightly music and the Guinness.

* * *

John especially loved the west coast, which was wild and empty, where no one lived and where the winds from the North Atlantic came racing in.

'Next stop, New York,' John said to himself as he stood looking out into the empty sea. It was near the end of their week on the island and he had come for one last long walk alone, from one end of the island to the other. From the north end where the cliffs were high and it was impossible to reach the beach, to the more gentle south where the sheep ate the grass, keeping it as short and tidy as on a golf course.

He loved this place. He had walked now for almost three hours and had seen hundreds of birds carried on the wind, diving into the sea for fish. He had also seen hundreds of sheep that ran away with frightened cries before he even came close to them. He had not seen a single person on his walk. True, he had looked down on to a small, golden beach and had seen two bicycles lying on the sand with two sets of footprints going away from them towards the bottom of the cliff as if two young lovers were looking for a quiet place.

But he had not seen anyone. That was why he now stopped and looked at the person in black who was sitting on the rocks near the sea. John was perhaps two hundred metres away from the person so it was difficult to see if it was a man or a woman. The person was dressed in a black suit and had either very short hair or no hair at all, but from this distance that was all John could see. He, if it was a man, was sitting totally still, looking out to sea but not moving his head, not moving at all. John stood and watched the man and then he too turned towards the sea, in the direction the man was looking. He could see nothing and when he turned back, the man had gone. Disappeared. Nothing surprising in that. There were so many places where he might have gone, hidden from view by the rocks. Maybe the man had noticed John and had decided to look for a place where he would be completely alone. John could understand that. He was looking for the same thing. He just hoped that the man would not come near the pool, *his* pool.

The pool was a rock pool, just a few metres from the ocean's edge. It was filled and refilled every day by the ocean as the waves broke over the rocks. John had found it on a previous visit when he had been on the island by himself. He had been walking for hours when he came to the pool and his feet were hot and tired. He had sat down beside the pool on a rock.

At first he had taken off only his boots and socks and rested his feet in the cool quiet water. It was wonderfully cold and inviting. John then looked around to make sure there was no one around and then he took off all his clothes and climbed slowly into the pool. He didn't swim much as the pool was small. Instead he lay on his back looking at the few small white clouds racing across the open sky.

Then he turned over on his face for a moment, his eyes open, his mouth closed, his arms hanging below him in the water, not moving, almost as if he were dead. As this thought went through John's head he turned over in the water, afraid that someone might walk past the pool and see him and think he was dead.

Now, as he came to the pool again, he took off his

clothes and climbed in, as he had done the first time. Then, as before, he dried himself with his cotton shirt and lay down on some grass near the pool and went to sleep. But this time his sleep would not be so restful.

Chapter 9

Sleeping by the pool

He woke in the cottage, although at first he did not know where he was. He lay still for a moment. It was very dark and he could not see much. He knew where he was only by the smells, the smell of the dried earth they burn in the fire places in the west of Ireland and the smell of the sheets, fresh from drying outside in the wind. But it was still difficult to see. There were no street lights on the island, no lights from street advertisements, no car lights going past. There was a darkness and a silence that you never get in the town. It was one of the things that John loved about the island.

But as he woke now, he did not feel comfortable. He did not like the darkness of the room where he lay. It made him feel nervous. He felt something was not quite right. Slowly, from the darkness, he began to recognise shapes: the lighter-coloured walls and the dark shapes of the heavy furniture in the cottage— the large wardrobe at the end of the bed where they put their clothes and where they could have put twice as many clothes, the painting on the wall of the two men on the beach pushing their little boat into the high waves of the Atlantic.

As he began to realise where he was, he also knew that something was very wrong. The room was quiet. Quieter than it should be. He could hear only the outside noises of the sea and a wind that whispered through the windows of the cottage. There were no noises from inside the cottage. He reached over in the bed towards Rachel, but knew already before his hand touched the cold sheets that she was not there. He sat up in bed and tried to say her name but nothing came out. He tried to shout but nothing came. His breathing was fast and very loud. He pulled the sheets back and threw them off the bed and saw that it was still empty. He got out of bed and ran to the wardrobe and opened it and looked inside it. Then he ran to the window and pulled back the curtains. He looked out into the darkness, pushing his face against the cold wet window and silently called Rachel's name. He could see no one outside. He turned to the little bed where Patrick lay and tried to scream again as he saw that that bed was empty too.

He ran to the living room, pushing and kicking at the furniture that got in his way. He screamed her name and this time it came out; from the bottom of his stomach the name came and he put his hands to his ears to stop it. It hurt so much to hear her name when she was not there, when she had gone.

He ran to the front door and pulled at it but it did not move. The key was in the lock and he turned it. But it simply turned and turned and the lock did not move. He ran back to the bedroom and stopped suddenly as he saw that the wardrobe door was opening. It opened slowly and someone stepped out. It was someone in black. The white of the face was the only light in the room. It was impossible to see if it was a man or a woman. It was carrying something. It spoke. The voice was the man's from the boat.

'The baby's fine. Don't worry.' And John saw that the man was holding Patrick.

John tried to speak but his mouth was dry and he could not produce any words but he heard the questions as if someone else was asking them.

'What are you...who are you? What are you doing with my son? Where is...?'

'The boy is fine,' the man said. 'It's all right. He'll

be OK now. They don't really die, you know, they come back. The little ones who go before their time. They come back from the other side. They always come back to us. They always come back.'

'What! What are you talking about? What do you mean, come back? What other side? What are you talking about? You mean death? My son is fine. He's not dead! Are you mad? And...' John looked around the room again. 'And...where is my wife? What have you done to my wife?'

John was trying to look into the man's face but it was still difficult to see anything. He noticed that the man's hair was very short but that was all he could see. The man spoke again. He spoke with a voice that was gentle and soft.

'Her work is done now. She can go back to the other side. You can let her go now. She has done very well. Look at the boy. The boy is fine. A lovely child.'

John looked at Patrick asleep in the man's arms and reached out to take him but as he put out his arms he felt himself start to fall backwards. Slowly at first, very slowly. The man was still speaking. His mouth formed the words but John could no longer hear the words. And now John felt as if he was falling faster and faster. But the man still stood there and did not seem any further away. With his whole body John knew that he was falling, even though nothing around him moved. He reached out again with his arms. The man too was reaching out his hand. Although John was still falling the hand came closer and closer, and finally it touched the side of his face. Everything stopped, then suddenly everything went dark.

Chapter 10
Dreams untold, dreams told

Rachel was bending over John, touching his face. He opened his eyes. He could see her mouth moving but he could hear nothing and then slowly her words came to him.

'John? John? Are you OK? I was going crazy with worry. You were gone for hours. What happened? You look terrible. I was frightened. I thought something had happened to you. Are you OK? What happened? John, speak to me!'

His throat was very dry and he found it difficult to say anything, but finally he managed to speak.

'Where am I? Where's Patrick?'

He sat up and looked around him. He was still beside the pool. Slowly he began to remember where he was. The sun was much lower in the sky now than when he had fallen asleep.

'I fell asleep. I had a dream. It was terrible. A terrible dream, a nightmare. It was awful. I thought you'd gone away. I thought you'd left me. I couldn't find you. I looked everywhere. It was awful. Oh God, it was awful. And the man had Patrick. Patrick! Where is he? Where's Patrick?'

'He's fine. He's fine, my love. Mrs Reagan is looking after him.'

'Mrs Reagan?'

'Yes, you know, the woman from the pub. He's fine. He's fine.' She pulled him close to her and held him tight. She pushed her face against his hair and held him. She held him as he cried. He cried as she had never seen him cry before.

'I thought you'd gone,' he said. 'I thought you'd gone.'

He repeated the words over and over again between his tears.

She held him tightly for a long time until slowly his tears stopped, although his whole body was still shaking. And then slowly she helped him to his feet and they began to walk away from the pool. They walked towards the path that led to the other side of the island and back to the cottages.

They didn't speak as they walked but she could feel the strength slowly returning to his body. She was no longer helping him to walk but was just holding his arm with her hand. She needed to hold him now as much as he needed to be held by her. As they came towards the cottages and the first pub they turned to each other.

'I thought I'd lost you.'

'I thought I'd lost you.'

They spoke the words together. Both of them. The same words at the same moment. And then they fell into each other's arms and held each other, and this time they were both crying. They stood like that for some time. They stood still like the people in a painting that hung in one of the local pubs. A painting of a man and a woman holding each other and crying, as if one of them was going away for a long time, for ever perhaps.

This island had seen many goodbyes like this as the men had left to find work in England or America. They made their promises to return soon or to send money so that the women could join them. Sometimes the money arrived, sometimes not even a letter arrived.

Sometimes the man came back.

'I'm OK now, honestly,' John said as Rachel pulled back from him a little and looked up into his face questioningly. 'Really,' he continued, 'it was a dream. It was a terrible dream but it was just a dream. I'm OK. I'm OK. I think maybe I was more tired than I thought I was. It was only a dream. I'm OK. Really, I'm OK.'

* * *

They returned to the pub and found Patrick playing happily with Mrs Reagan.

'Ah, he's a lovely boy! He's a darling. I could keep him for myself. It's a pleasure to look after him. It really is. You know, next time you come you must stay here at the pub and I can look after him for you.'

'Have you got a room?' John asked.

'Sure, you know we have rooms, John.'

'No, I mean, do you have a free room now? For this coming week?'

'John? We're going back tomorrow,' Rachel reminded him.

'I know, but I think maybe I need a longer rest. I don't want to go back just yet. I could phone the office and tell them I'm taking another week's holiday. What do you think? And look at Patrick. He's enjoying this so much. He's not going to get the chance to see much sand or sea in London, is he? And he's so safe here, isn't he? No traffic, nothing. Come on, what do you say? Shall we stay?'

'But after your...after that...are you sure you want to stay after...?'

'It was a dream, Rachel, it was a horrible dream but it was only a dream. I've had a few bad dreams recently but that was only a dream, nothing else. I dreamt I had lost you...' His voice almost broke again. He took a deep breath and then he finished his thought. 'And now I just want to stay here for another week and have some time with you. I don't want to go back to work just yet.'

* * *

And so they stayed a second week on the island, but not in the cottage. They moved to the pub, to a room above the bar. It was certainly more noisy, especially at nights. The island pubs seemed to close when they wanted and they never wanted to until three o'clock in the morning. But Patrick slept through it all and John preferred the noise to the silence now. He and Rachel often joined the crowd downstairs in the pub for the singing and the 'crack', as the Irish call good conversation, and Mrs Reagan was always happy to look after Patrick.

'I'd rather look after this darling boy than listen to these old fools talking,' she had said looking at her husband and his brother who also worked in the pub, and they had all laughed.

But after the pub closed John still found it difficult to go to sleep and he hated it if he woke up in the darkness. It reminded him too much of his dream. When he did go to bed he lay close to Rachel rather than facing away from her, as he usually did when they slept together. He liked to be close enough to her to feel her breathing.

They had not talked any more about his nightmare. John did not want to. He wanted to forget about it. He wanted especially to forget what the man in black had said about Patrick and about Rachel. He wanted to forget this dream as he was already trying to forget the story of the hitch-hiker in white. He wanted to forget all that. He just wanted to hold on to his wife. He realised that for the first time in their marriage there were things that he was not telling Rachel. He did not like it but he did not want to talk about these things.

He lay beside Rachel, his hand resting on her stomach, feeling it rise and fall with her sleeping breath. He didn't want to let go of her. He was almost afraid to fall asleep.

As the week went on, however, he began to relax and stopped looking nervously over his shoulder every time the pub door opened. But he didn't go on any more long walks by himself. They walked mainly down to the nearby beach where Patrick was discovering the pleasure of sand. It was a full-time job for John to keep the sand out of Patrick's mouth, hair, eyes and other parts of the body. He enjoyed having the time to spend with his son and he promised himself that he would spend more time with Patrick in the future and less time at work.

On the last night he and Rachel went together for a walk, leaving Patrick with Mrs Reagan. It was the first time they had been out together without Patrick on this holiday. They walked to the end of the island where a large fishing boat had washed up on the rocks fifteen years before. It was an amazing sight. This large boat was sitting on the rocks fifty metres from the sea. It had sat in the same place since it had been caught in a storm and the waves had thrown it onto the rocks.

'It's amazing, isn't it? It's like a big toy. Patrick would love this,' said John walking around the boat and looking up at it. 'They didn't have the money to get it moved back to the sea, so they just left it here. Amazing.'

He was still looking up at the boat when Rachel spoke softly behind him.

'I want to tell you about my dream. About the dream I had before Patrick's birthday. Remember?'

John nodded.

'I can tell you about it now. Now that we're here and now that his birthday is over. Now I feel he's safe, you know.'

'Are you sure?'

'Yes. I want to. It was terrible. Like your dream, but I want to talk about it now.'

She sat down and John sat beside her, their backs against the side of the boat and she began.

'I had the dream three or four times. I dreamt I was with a child, but it wasn't Patrick. He was very like Patrick, but it wasn't him. And we were getting ready for his birthday party. He was sitting behind me on the floor and was playing with a toy car and making noises, making car noises. And I felt really happy. I had this lovely warm feeling inside, and I knew I had never been happier, and I was singing to myself and smiling...and...'

John put his arm around Rachel and she smiled at him and nodded but the smile did not come easily this time.

'And then,' she continued, 'then it all changed. Suddenly I felt something was wrong and I wanted to turn round and look at him but I couldn't...I couldn't turn round. I couldn't even turn my head to look at him. And then I realised that the noises I was hearing were not his car noises any more. They were not the car noises he was making. They were real car noises and it was suddenly dark and I wasn't in the house and I was...I don't know where I was. And then the car noises got louder and louder and there was a scream and a crash and the world seemed to be turning over and over and I couldn't see the baby and...and then I woke up. I had this same dream again and again and again, and I was getting really frightened. I was afraid something was going to happen to Patrick. I don't know what. But I was afraid of cars. I was afraid to be near them. I was afraid something was going to happen to Patrick before his birthday. I was sure something bad was going to happen before his birthday. It was awful. But it's OK now. He's safe. We're all safe, aren't we? And everything's fine now, isn't it? It was just a dream, wasn't it? Just like yours was a dream. My dream didn't mean anything. And yours didn't mean anything either. Did it?'

John kept his arms around Rachel as she pushed her face against his chest. He held her in his arms.

'It's all right now,' he said.

Rachel couldn't see his face, couldn't see the

expression on his face. His face had turned white again and he looked frightened. He was remembering the policeman's story of the car accident and of the baby that had died. He was remembering what the man in black had said about a baby 'coming back from the other side'. He was remembering the man's story of the hitch-hiker on the road from Brighton. And now Rachel's dream about a baby in a car accident!

'It's all right now,' he said again. 'It's all right.'

But John wasn't sure that he believed what he was saying. He wasn't sure he believed his own words.

Chapter 11
Stop it! Stop it!

John stood in their bedroom at home. It was Sunday evening. They had returned from Ireland the day before and now John was getting ready for work the next day. He always got his clothes ready the night before. It gave him an extra few minutes in bed the next morning. An extra few minutes to lie close to Rachel in the warmth before he had to get up and go to work. He took his dark blue jacket out of the wardrobe. He held it against himself and stood in front of the mirror. It was a jacket he often wore to work. He looked at himself. He looked relaxed and suntanned after their two-week holiday.

But he did not feel relaxed. He'd felt relaxed for a while in the middle of the holiday, but Rachel's dream had brought back all his fears. There were so many questions he could not answer about the dreams and the stories of the policeman and the man on the cassette. They were questions he did not even want to think about. But he could not forget them.

He picked up his wallet from the table beside

the bed and put it into his jacket pocket. There was something already in his pocket. A box. It felt like a cigarette packet but that wasn't possible. He had stopped smoking over ten years before. But now he almost hoped it was a packet of cigarettes. Now he felt he wanted a cigarette. Now he felt he needed a cigarette. He took the thing out of his pocket and looked at it. It was an audio cassette box. He opened it. There was a cassette inside. Nothing was written on the cassette and, for a moment, he wondered what it was and then he remembered.

The last time he had worn this jacket was his last day at work. The day Jenny and he had driven down to Brighton. And this was the cassette they had listened to in his office. The cassette from the radio station with the story of the lady in white. He must have put it in his pocket when they left his office that Friday.

John stood and looked at the cassette in his hand and all the feelings he'd had that day came back to him now. His mouth was suddenly very dry and his stomach seemed to drop to his feet.

'John, dinner's ready. Are you coming down?' It was Rachel calling from downstairs.

'I'm coming,' he answered.

He looked at the cassette in his hand. He put it down on the table beside the bed but then picked it up again immediately. He didn't want Rachel to find it. Instead he put it back in his pocket and went downstairs. He would do something with it later.

They had dinner together. John was very quiet while they ate but this did not surprise Rachel. He was often like this at the end of a holiday. He enjoyed his work but he found it difficult to go back to it after a holiday. The last night after a holiday was usually difficult for him, so she did not say anything about his silence.

They went to bed early and Rachel fell asleep quickly, as she always did. She always slept well, but she woke up immediately if Patrick made any noise at all. Tonight Patrick was sleeping very quietly.

John, however, could not sleep. Seeing the cassette again had brought back the whole story of the lady in white. He could almost hear the man's voice in his head telling the story, telling the man's story, telling John's story. Rachel lay quietly beside him. John did not reach out to touch her as he normally did when he woke in the middle of the night. Pictures filled his head like a film playing too fast, like one film mixed up with another. Pictures of Rachel dressed in white on the cliffs in Ireland mixed with words from the story about the hitch-hiker. Pictures of Rachel standing on a lonely road near Brighton mixed with pictures and noises of cars crashing. Pictures of their bedroom in Ireland and the words of a man dressed in black. Words about Patrick 'coming back from the other side' and 'her work is done. She can go back to the other side now'.

John was becoming hotter and hotter as he lay in bed. His thoughts jumped from place to place, but he sat up immediately and went cold when he heard the scream.

He sat in bed listening. Rachel did not move. He heard nothing, only Rachel's quiet breathing. He went quickly to Patrick's room and looked down at the child's bed. Patrick was also sleeping quietly. He looked out of the window. There was no one. There had been no scream that anyone else could hear. The scream, like the pictures, was all in his head. He stood watching Patrick. Patrick was quiet, but was he safe? Was Rachel safe? He walked slowly to the wardrobe and opened the door as he had done in his dream. He looked through the clothes. He did not know what or who he was looking for. There were clothes, only clothes.

John went into the next bedroom and sat on the bed there with his head in his hands and closed his eyes and tried to see nothing.

'What is going on here? What is happening to me? What is happening to me? Am I going mad? What does this all mean? Oh God, help me, help me. Please help me, I don't understand any of this.'

He sat with his head in his hands and cried softly to himself.

He must have slept a few hours because when he opened his eyes again it was already light. He washed and dressed without waking Rachel. He left the house without waking her. He did not touch her or kiss her goodbye, as he usually did. He just got into his car and drove off.

Slowly, as he drove, his thoughts began to become calmer. In the daylight things seemed different. The night before began to seem like another bad dream. His worst fears and worries always came in the middle of the night. In the morning he looked back and could not believe how he had felt, what he had done in the night. 'There is an explanation to all of this,' he thought.

He began to think of work and his mood began to improve. It was a beautiful morning and John enjoyed driving—the beauty of the morning was helping to push away the dark thoughts of his sleepless night. He began to relax and to look forward to getting back to work. He turned on the cassette player in the car and pushed the play button. It was a cassette with some of his favourite Irish songs. The song that was playing was painfully sad.

Hillhall, Ireland
Eighteen ninety

My dear and loving son, John
I'm sorry to bring you
The very sad news
That your dear old mother
Has passed on
We buried her down by
The river in Moira
Beside your young brother Tom

John started to cry, gently. He thought of his own mother who had died four years before. Before he had met Rachel. He could see his mother's face in front of him. He could see the small church where they had held the funeral service for her. He began to cry now as he had cried when his mother had died. He tried to dry his eyes with the back of his hand as he continued to look at the road ahead of him.

As he dried his eyes, the music disappeared and John heard the voice of the man instead, telling the story of the hitch-hiker, of the lady in white. John looked at the cassette player. A man's voice was coming from it now. It was the man's voice from the radio programme.

I just wanted to get her out of the car. I said, 'We'll soon be there,' but she didn't answer. Then suddenly, as I was getting close to a bend in the road, she started to scream. I went cold inside...

John hit the stop button on the cassette player but the voice continued.

...and my stomach jumped and she was screaming, 'Oh God, we're losing control, we're losing control, watch out, watch out, oh my God!'

John pressed a button on the cassette player and the cassette jumped out, but the voice continued. John started shouting to cover the sound of the other voice. He did not want to hear this story again.

'Stop it, stop it. I don't want to hear this. Do you hear me! Stop it. Stop it. I've had enough of this!' John shouted and hit the cassette player with his left hand. The tears filled John's eyes. The voice continued.

...and she was looking at me. She was looking at me... it's difficult to describe the look but...I don't know what it was, it was like she was trying to see what kind of person I was. It was, I don't know, it was almost sexy and yet uncertain, as if she didn't know if she could trust me or not. I mean, after the tears and everything, it made me feel sort of excited and nervous at the same time. And a bit uncomfortable.

John could hardly see the road in front of him.

'Stop it! Stop it! Stop it!' he shouted and hit blindly at the cassette player with his left hand. His whole body was shaking now and he was shouting non-stop.

'Stop it! Stop it! Stop it! Stop it! I don't want to hear this again. This is not about me. Do you understand? This is nothing to do with me. This is not my story. Stop it, stop it! Leave me alone. Please. Please leave us alone!'

Behind him a car was blowing its horn and flashing its lights. A car coming towards John was also flashing its lights. John hardly noticed through his tears. And then suddenly he realised that the voice had stopped. He also realised that his car was going wildly from one side of the road to the other. He heard for the first time the horn of the car behind him and saw the flashing lights of the cars coming towards him.

He pulled his car over to the side of the road and stopped. The car that had been travelling behind drove past. The driver turned to look at John and pointed to his head with his fingers as if to say, 'Are you mad?'

John didn't notice him. As his car had come to a stop, he put his head in his hands and started to cry violently.

Chapter 12
Don't look back

John sat for some time in his car and then drove to work. He sat in his office but he could not think about work. The success of his television programmes seemed empty now. He got back into his car and drove around London for hours. Once or twice he saw road signs for Brighton. He stopped his car and looked at the signs. He thought about driving back to the village. But it was getting dark and he decided to go home instead.

He was not looking forward to going home. When he arrived home dinner was ready. John was quiet as they ate.

'Are you OK, John? You're very quiet. Is anything the matter? Did something happen at the office?'

'I'm fine,' he said. 'You know I always find it difficult going back to work.'

'Are you worried about something? You've been so quiet since that last day in Ireland. If there was something wrong you would tell me, wouldn't you? John? You would tell me?'

'Yes, of course. But I'm fine. I'm fine. It's just going back to work, you know.'

He stood up and walked around the table towards her. She thought he was going to kiss her, but instead he just put his hand on her shoulder.

'I'm fine. Really.'

Rachel went to bed early but John stayed up.

'There's a programme on TV I want to see,' he said.

When he did go to bed later he couldn't get to sleep. He was almost afraid to go to sleep. Afraid of what he might dream. And he didn't feel comfortable lying beside Rachel. He went to the next room again and slept a little. At breakfast Rachel asked him again what the matter was. They had never slept in separate beds before in this house. But John only said that he was thinking about work and could not sleep. That it was nothing important. That there was nothing wrong.

They both knew, for the first time, that there was something unspoken between them. But John could not say more. How could he tell her about the strange thoughts that raced through his head as he lay in the middle of the night in the darkness?

'I'll be working late this evening,' he said. 'I did almost no work yesterday. You know what it's like at work on the first day after a holiday. I'll be back late. Don't make dinner for me.'

John got into his car and drove off but he didn't go to work. He drove around for hours again and then finally he took the road for Brighton and went back to the village where he had first met Rachel and where the three men had met the hitch-hiker.

He sat there in his car for hours and then went home. But the next night he came back to the village again, and then, on the third night, he was back again, sitting in his car at the exact place where he had first met Rachel.

On the first night he had come here he had seen nothing. But on the second night something appeared suddenly in the rear view mirror of his car. John's hair stood on end. He heard footsteps beside the car but he continued to look straight ahead. Then the footsteps moved on and he heard a dog. He relaxed as a man walked past with the dog, but then the man stopped. He looked back towards the car, bending down a little as he tried to look inside. John waved but the man was obviously wondering who was sitting here alone in a car late at night. The man walked on but returned a few minutes later on the other side of the road. Then the man started to cross the road and walk towards the car. John started the engine quickly and drove off. He did not want to explain to the man what he was doing. He had no explanation that would make any sense. He did not really know why he had to come back again.

And now John sat in his car in the village for the third night. It was a wet night and the car which had been warm after his journey, was now getting very cold. The inside of the car windows was wet from his breath and it was getting difficult to see anything clearly through them. He cleaned the windows with the arm of his jacket. There was not much to see. The road that went up the hill in front of him was empty and dark. There were no street lights in front of him and the ones behind him from the village did not come this far. The road was empty in both directions. He had been sitting here for half an hour already and only two or three cars had passed. He cleaned the rear view mirror again and turned on the heater in the back window. The window slowly began to clear and he could see out. He could see the road behind more clearly now in the mirror. A few lights from some of the houses helped the street lights. He could see the first house behind him quite clearly. The two front windows were lit up and he thought he could see someone sitting inside but maybe it was just a piece of furniture. An armchair perhaps. The other houses were only dark shapes behind him, nothing more. He shook with the cold and he asked himself what he was doing here, why he had come back to the village again and again.

He had been here for three nights already. No one had come. No lady in white. Is that who he expected? Did he think she came here every night, this mysterious hitch-hiker? And if she did come, if she did come tonight, what then? Well, then he would know, wouldn't he? Then, one way or another he would know. Either it would be as Jenny had said, a woman looking for her memory, or... Who else could it be? Rachel? Did he really think it could be Rachel? Did he really think that this lady in white was Rachel?

And if this lady in white didn't come? If no one came, as no one had come the first night, and no one had come the second night. What then? Would he continue to drive half-way to Brighton from London, park here and wait, wait until another villager saw him and called the police? Wait here for how many nights? And if no one ever came, what would that mean? This was madness. This was completely mad. This was not helping him get back to a normal life.

This would destroy him, this would...

There was a flash of white in the rear mirror. He thought at first it was a light and he looked again deep into the mirror but the white was still there. The white of a dress. A woman in white. A woman in white was standing just behind the car, not moving. He could see only part of her body. He could not see her legs, he could not see her head, or face. Because of where she was standing he could only see part of her in the rear-view mirror. He did not want to turn around and look at her. He was afraid. He looked into the side mirror and could see a little more. Yes, a woman. It was definitely a woman. But he could still not see the head, nor the face. He felt even colder inside now. His stomach suddenly felt very empty. His hands felt as if they were stuck to the steering wheel. He could not move and she did not move. And then suddenly she took a step forward and John watched her disappear from the rear-view mirror. He looked at the side mirror as she took another step forward. 'Oh God, what is going on?' he whispered to himself.

The woman moved forward and then stopped beside the car, beside the passenger door. John turned and looked. The dress was close to the window now and he heard a noise as her hand reached down for the handle of the door. The handle moved, but the door was locked and John did not move to open it. Her hand came up and rested on the window. Her right hand. He looked at her hand. There were no rings on her long suntanned fingers. She lifted one finger as if to knock on the window or maybe to write something on the wet glass and then the hand moved away and she also moved back from the car. She moved slowly so more of her body could be seen through the window. She stepped back a little more, and he could see more and then she took another step and John could see her neck and then...

John drove almost a kilometre without turning the car lights on. He had started the engine and, as the woman had stepped back, the car had jumped forward and he had looked straight ahead and was gone, five hundred metres down the road even before he knew what he was doing.

He didn't look back. He wasn't going to look back. He was not going to look back along this road and he was not going to look back on anything that had happened over the last month or so. He remembered, for the last time he told himself, the dream he'd had on the island. He didn't want to lose his wife. He wasn't going to lose his wife. He was certainly not going to lose her as a result of the madness his own mind had been making over the last few weeks.

He drove on. There was no other traffic on the road and he drove faster than was safe on such a dark, wet night. It seemed as dark as it had been in the cottage in Ireland. As dark as it had been in his dream.

He had driven almost thirty kilometres from the village in less than twenty minutes when he noticed something in his rear view mirror. There seemed to be a light coming from the back seat of the car. He slowed down and turned around to look at the back seat.

His mobile phone was lying on the seat and the light was coming from it. The phone. He could phone Rachel. She would be at home. He thought again of the lady in white whose face he hadn't wanted to see. That had been twenty minutes ago. That woman had not been Rachel. Rachel was at home. He could phone her now and she would answer. He stopped the car at the side of the road and picked up the phone.

He sat for a minute looking at it. It would take him another thirty minutes to drive home, even driving as fast as he was. No one could have driven from the village to their house and arrived there by now. It was impossible. He could phone Rachel now and she would be at home and he would know that the lady in white was someone else. And still he could only sit and look at the phone and his fears returned.

And then he called his home number. The phone rang. No one answered. It continued to ring and then he heard a voice. It was his own voice on the answer machine.

'I'm sorry that Rachel and John are not here to take your call at the moment but if you would like to...'

His eyes filled with tears again and he could hardly breath and then suddenly the message stopped and he could hear Rachel's voice.

'Hello...' Her voice was sleepy.

'Rachel?'

'John? Where are you? Are you all right? I was sleeping when the phone rang.'

'I'm fine, my love. I'm on my way home now. I'll be there in about half an hour. Will you wait up for me?

'Of course I will.'

'Rachel?'

'Yes.'

'I love you.'

'I love you too, John. Come home soon.'

'I will...I will.'

He started the car for the journey home and he would not look back until he got there.

After reading

读后活动

Choose some of these activities.

1. Which chapter do you remember most clearly from *The Lady in White*? Why?

2. Do you think that John will make the TV series on urban myths after his experience? Why or why not?

3. Do you think *The Lady in White* is a good title? Why or why not? Make up an alternative.

4. On page 107, John asks Rachel: 'Will you wait up for me?' Write the conversation between John and Rachel when he arrives home.

5. Imagine you are writing a book about urban myths. Write the first page of the book.

6. Imagine you are John on holiday on Inishbofin. Write a postcard to Jenny in London.

7. Make your own activities for other students to do, e.g. make a word search puzzle.

Learning guide|学习指导

Chapter 1

New words 生词

- diet /ˈdaɪət/ *n.* 饮食
- documentary /ˌdɒkjuˈmentri/ *a.* 纪实的，记录的
- excitement /ɪkˈsaɪtmənt/ *n.* 兴奋
- fantastic /fænˈtæstɪk/ *a.* 极好的
- frightened /ˈfraɪtnd/ *a.* 恐惧的
- hired /haɪəd/ *a.* 租的
- meditation /ˌmedɪˈteɪʃn/ *n.* 沉思，冥想
- overlook /ˌəʊvəˈlʊk/ *v.* 俯视
- pause /pɔːz/ *v.* 暂停
- relationship /rɪˈleɪʃnʃɪp/ *n.* 关系
- scream /skriːm/ *v.* 尖叫
- yoga /ˈjəʊɡə/ *n.* 瑜伽

Phrases & expressions 短语和表达

- a series of... 一系列……
- documentary programme 纪录片
- managing director 总经理
- pleasure boat 游船

📖 Cultural notes 文化点滴

• River Thames: 泰晤士河。英国著名的"母亲河",沿岸有许多著名景点,如伦敦塔桥、伦敦眼和英国议会大厦等。泰晤士河的入海口热闹繁忙,然而其上游的河道则以静态之美著称于世。在英国历史上,泰晤士河流域占有举足轻重的地位。

• The Houses of Parliament: 英国议会大厦,又称"威斯敏斯特宫"。位于伦敦中心、泰晤士河西岸,是英国议会(包括上议院和下议院)的所在地。

• Tower Bridge: 伦敦塔桥。位于英国伦敦,横跨泰晤士河,将伦敦南北区连接成整体,因在伦敦塔附近而得名。该桥是一座上开悬索桥,始建于 1886 年,1894 年 6 月 30 日对公众开放。

🔍 Reading exercises 阅读练习

1. Match the beginnings and endings.

_____ 1) John's new television series

_____ 2) John and his wife Rachel never

_____ 3) Recently, John had become worried

_____ 4) Rachel wouldn't talk to him

_____ 5) Rachel was frightened

a) kept any secrets from each other.

b) about the bad dreams that woke her.

c) had been a great success.

d) of taking Patrick in a car.

e) about his wife's strange behaviour.

2. Why do you think Rachel is frightened for Patrick's safety?

Chapter 2

🔍 New words 生词

- book /bʊk/ *v.* 预订
- cliff /klɪf/ *n.* 悬崖
- disappointed /ˌdɪsəˈpɔɪntɪd/ *a.* 失望的
- evidence /ˈevɪdəns/ *n.* 证据
- hitch-hiker /hɪtʃ ˈhaɪkə(r)/ *n.* 搭便车的人
- mysterious /mɪˈstɪəriəs/ *a.* 神秘的
- petrol /ˈpetrəl/ *n.* 汽油
- suggestion /səˈdʒestʃən/ *n.* 建议
- thoughtfully /ˈθɔːtfəli/ *ad.* 若有所思地
- warn /wɔːn/ *v.* 警告

🔍 Phrases & expressions 短语和表达

- run out of... 用完……
- urban myth 都市神话

🔍 Cultural notes 文化点滴

• Cliffs of Moher: 莫赫悬崖。位于爱尔兰岛西海岸，是欧洲最高的悬崖。莫赫悬崖是爱尔兰最重要的海鸟栖息地，同时悬崖上还生长着许多珍稀植物。

• St Paul's Cathedral: 圣保罗大教堂。巴洛克风格建筑的代表，以其壮观的穹顶闻名世界。

🔍 Reading exercise 阅读练习

1. Put the events in the right order.

_____ a) John remembered how he had first met Rachel.

_____ b) Rachel even suggested hiring a car.

_____ c) John and Jenny talked about his idea for a new TV series.

_____ d) Rachel sounded happy and excited about the holiday on the phone.

_____ e) John and Jenny had lunch together.

2. Has anyone ever told you an urban myth?

(Chapter 3)

🔍 New words 生词

- cassette /kəˈset/ *n.* 磁带，录音带
- cottage /ˈkɒtɪdʒ/ *n.* 乡间小别墅，小屋
- cover /ˈkʌvə(r)/ *v.* 报道
- heater /ˈhiːtə(r)/ *n.* 加热器
- interviewer /ˈɪntəvjuːə(r)/ *n.* 采访者
- still /stɪl/ *a.* 静止的

🔍 Phrases & expressions 短语和表达

- cassette player 盒式磁带录音机
- disagree with... 不赞同……
- stand on end 立起来
- stare at... 盯着……看

🔍 Cultural notes 文化点滴

• Brighton: 布赖顿。英格兰南部的海滨城市，以其密布鹅卵石的海滩著称。

• Cambridge: 剑桥。英国剑桥郡的首府，位于伦敦北部，是剑桥大学所在地。

• Glasgow: 格拉斯哥。位于苏格兰西部的克莱德河河口，是苏格兰最大的城市。

• Halloween: 万圣节前夜。在每年的 10 月 31 日，是西方的传统节日。

• Liverpool: 利物浦。位于英格兰西北部的默西河河口，是英国第二大商业港。

🔍 Reading exercise 阅读练习

True or false?

_____ a) Jenny found three very different stories.

_____ b) Each story happened in the same place.

_____ c) Each story was told by a man.

_____ d) The story happened on a wet, stormy night.

_____ e) The hitch-hiker said that she was all right.

(Chapter 4)

🔍 New words 生词

• bend /bend/ *n.* 拐弯

- blind /blaɪnd/ *v.* 使目眩，使眼花
- blow /bləʊ/ *v.* 鸣响
- brake /breɪk/ *n.* 刹车
- embarrassed /ɪmˈbærəst/ *a.* 难为情的
- handle /ˈhændl/ *n.* 把手
- horn /hɔːn/ *n.* 喇叭
- relive /ˌriːˈlɪv/ *v.* 重温
- situation /ˌsɪtʃuˈeɪʃn/ *n.* 场合，情况
- slim /slɪm/ *a.* 苗条的
- strength /streŋθ/ *n.* 力量
- stuck /stʌk/ *a.* 卡住的
- whisper /ˈwɪspə(r)/ *v.* 低声说

Phrases & expressions 短语和表达

- be about to do... 打算做……
- kind of... 有点儿……
- manage to do... 设法做成……
- steering wheel 方向盘
- take a deep breath 深呼吸

Reading exercises 阅读练习

1. Complete the summary.

The driver noticed how _____ the hitch-hiker was and wondered why she was _____ . When she turned to look at him, he felt _____ and _____ but also uncomfortable. As the car came near a bend, she started _____ , saying 'We're losing _____ !' Then she started _____ the steering wheel. The man was surprised how _____ she was and _____ her. There was almost a terrible _____ . When the car stopped, he could see _____ on her face.

2. Why do you think John said: 'No, it wasn't like that'? (page 30).

Chapter 5

🔍 New words 生词

- agreement /əˈgriːmənt/ *n.* 协议
- competition /ˌkɒmpɪˈtɪʃn/ *n.* 竞争
- disbelief /ˌdɪsbɪˈliːf/ *n.* 怀疑
- helplessly /ˈhelpləsli/ *ad.* 无助地
- motorway /ˈməʊtəweɪ/ *n.*（英）高速公路
- recognise /ˈrekəgnaɪz/ *v.* 认出
- remind /rɪˈmaɪnd/ *v.* 提醒
- retold /ˌriːˈtəʊld/ *v.* 复述
- roundabout /ˈraʊndəbaʊt/ *n.* 环形交叉路口
- sign /saɪn/ *v.* 签字
- speeding /ˈspiːdɪŋ/ *a.* 高速行驶的

🔍 Phrases & expressions 短语和表达

- break down 发生故障
- prime minister 总理
- pull out（汽车或列车）开出
- rear-view mirror 后视镜
- side mirror 侧后视镜

🔍 Cultural notes 文化点滴

· Croydon: 克罗伊顿。英国大伦敦南部的一个区。

- Hitler: 阿道夫·希特勒。奥地利裔德国人，纳粹党党魁，第二次世界大战的发动者。

- Neville Chamberlain: 亚瑟·内维尔·张伯伦（Arthur Neville Chamberlain，1869—1940）。英国政治家，1937 年到 1940 年任英国首相。他由于在第二次世界大战前夕对希特勒纳粹德国实行绥靖政策而备受谴责。绥靖政策是第二次世界大战加速的原因之一。

- Waterloo Bridge: 滑铁卢桥。英国伦敦一座跨越泰晤士河的桥梁，建于 1817 年。滑铁卢桥得名于 1815 年英国取得胜利的滑铁卢战役。

Reading exercise 阅读练习

True or false?

_____ a) Jenny wanted to know what John was thinking.

_____ b) John normally chatted a lot.

_____ c) John talked to Jenny on the journey.

_____ d) While John and Jenny were driving to the village, the car broke down.

_____ e) John knew the name of the village from the recording.

Chapter 6

New words 生词

- crash /kræʃ/ *n.* 撞车声
- gossip /ˈɡɒsɪp/ *v.* 传闲话
- incident /ˈɪnsɪdənt/ *n.* 事件

- marking /ˈmɑːkɪŋ/ *n.* 标志
- operator /ˈɒpəreɪtə(r)/ *n.* 接线员
- sink /sɪŋk/ *v.* 下沉，下陷
- suicide /ˈsuːɪsaɪd/ *v.* 自杀
- thoughtful /ˈθɔːtfl/ *a.* 沉思的；体贴的
- unspoken /ˌʌnˈspəʊkən/ *a.* 未说出口的

Reading exercises 阅读练习

1. Who...

      a) phoned the man who told the story on the recording?

      b) called the police?

      c) was a middle-aged man in his fifties?

      d) was silent and hardly moved?

      e) wondered about the family photos?

2. Correct the summary.

The accident happened on a fine, clear day. The car may have gone round a bend too fast and the driver lost control. There were two other cars involved in the crash. The police checked the car afterwards and found something wrong with the brakes and steering wheel. The two passengers in the car died in hospital—a woman and her baby girl.

Chapter 7

New words 生词

- break /ˈbreɪk/ *v.* (因激动) 变调
- coincidence /kəʊˈɪnsɪdəns/ *n.* 巧合

- drop /drɒp/ *v.* 放下
- exhausted /ɪɡˈzɔːstɪd/ *a.* 筋疲力尽的
- fail /feɪl/ *v.* 使失望
- relative /ˈrelətɪv/ *n.* 亲人
- scene /siːn/ *n.* 现场
- suntanned /sʌnˈtænd/ *a.* 被太阳晒黑的

Phrases & expressions 短语和表达

- for God's sake 看在上帝的分上
- have to do with... 与……有关
- look through... 浏览……
- petrol station 加油站
- Registry Office 登记处
- Tax Office 税务局

Cultural note 文化点滴

• Sahara Desert: 撒哈拉沙漠。约形成于 250 万年前，是世界第二大荒漠（仅次于南极洲），也是世界最大的沙质荒漠，位于非洲北部。该地区气候条件非常恶劣，是地球上最不适合生物生存的地方之一。

Reading exercises 阅读练习

Match the beginnings and endings.

_____ 1) The police tried to find friends and family

_____ 2) The police knew the dead woman had a sister

_____ 3) People remembered seeing a young woman near the car

_____ 4) The way John met Rachel was similar

_____ 5) Jenny told John not to worry about the stories

a) but she disappeared.

b) and enjoy the holiday with his family.

c) but had no idea where she could be.

d) of the woman who was killed.

e) to part of the story on the recording.

Chapter 8

New words 生词

- dive /daɪv/ _v._ 跳水
- inviting /ɪn'vaɪtɪŋ/ _a._ 吸引人的
- monument /'mɒnjumənt/ _n._ 墓碑
- peaceful /'piːsfl/ _a._ 平静的
- port /pɔːt/ _n._ 港口
- previous /'priːviəs/ _a._ 之前的
- restful /'restfl/ _a._ 平静悠闲的

Phrases & expressions 短语和表达

- golf course 高尔夫球场
- turn over 翻过来

Cultural notes 文化点滴

• Atlantic Ocean: 大西洋。世界第二大洋，占地球表面积的近 20%，平均深度 3627 米，最深处波多黎各海沟深达 9218 米。

• Guinness: 健力士黑啤，又称吉尼斯黑啤。世界第一大黑啤酒品牌，也是吉尼斯世界纪录的起源。

Reading exercises 阅读练习

1. Put the events in the right order.

　　＿＿＿ a) John remembered walking on the cliffs with Rachel.

　　＿＿＿ b) John went for his last long walk on the island.

　　＿＿＿ c) John was trying to forget about the lady in white.

　　＿＿＿ d) John watched a man in black, sitting near the sea.

　　＿＿＿ e) John looked for a place where he could be alone.

　　＿＿＿ f) A man on the boat spoke to John about dolphins.

2. 'But this time his sleep would not be so restful.' (page 74). What do you think will happen?

Chapter 9

Reading exercise 阅读练习

What happened in John's dream?

　　a) He could hear the sound of traffic.

　　b) He could hear the sound of the wind and sea.

　　c) A person appeared from the wardrobe with Patrick.

　　d) A person appeared from the wardrobe with Rachel.

　　e) John could see the man's face clearly.

　　f) The man's voice was gentle and soft.

Chapter 10

🔍 New words 生词

- darling /ˈdɑːlɪŋ/ *n.* 可爱的人；宝贝
- expression /ɪkˈspreʃn/ *n.* 表情

🔍 Phrase & expression 短语和表达

- turn over and over 不断翻滚

🔍 Reading exercises 阅读练习

1. Who said what?

_____ a) 'I was going crazy with worry.'

_____ b) 'It was terrible. A terrible dream, a nightmare.'

_____ c) 'I thought I'd lost you.'

_____ d) 'But after your…after that…are you sure you want to stay after…?'

_____ e) 'I'd rather look after this darling boy…'

2. The last line of Chapter 10 is: 'He wasn't sure he believed his own words.' What do you think John believes?

Chapter 11

🔍 New words 生词

- blindly /ˈblaɪndli/ *ad.* 盲目地
- flash /flæʃ/ *v.* 使闪光
- sleepless /ˈsliːpləs/ *a.* 无眠的

🔍 Phrases & expressions 短语和表达

- hit the stop button 按下停止按钮
- pull over 靠边停车
- mix up with... 与……混合

🔍 Reading exercise 阅读练习

Complete the summary.

After coming back from holiday, John did not feel _____. There were so many _____ he couldn't answer about the _____ and the stories. In his pocket, John was surprised to find a _____ with the story of the lady in white. He didn't want _____ to find it. During dinner, John was very _____. That night, he couldn't sleep. In the car, he heard the story of the lady in white. John became angry and drove so badly that there was almost an _____. He stopped his car and began to _____.

(Chapter 12)

🔍 Phrases & expressions 短语和表达

- make sense 讲得通
- stay up 熬夜
- stick to... 粘住……

🔍 Reading exercises 阅读练习

1. What happened on the night John saw the lady in white? Put the events in the right order.

　　＿＿＿ a) John drove away at top speed.

　　＿＿＿ b) John saw something white in the rear-view mirror.

　　＿＿＿ c) She moved towards the side of the car, and tried to open the passenger door.

　　＿＿＿ d) John spoke to Rachel on his mobile phone.

　　＿＿＿ e) Then he saw a woman in white standing behind his car.

　　＿＿＿ f) Now he knew Rachel was not the lady in white.

2. Who or what do you think the lady in white was?

Translation
参考译文

神秘搭车人

第 1 章　光明与黑暗

● 第5页

　　一个男人和一个女人互相拥抱着在办公室里跳舞。他们边跳边笑。他们手挽着手，跳呀跳，不想让这一刻结束。

　　"我们做到了，约翰。我们真的做到了。"

　　"我知道我们做到了，珍妮。我知道。"

　　约翰是一位电视节目制作人，而珍妮是他的助理。他们正在为一档由他们制作的六集电视系列节目而感到激动。这档系列节目叫作"了解你的思想，热爱你的身体"，是关于身体和思想之间的关系的。每一集都聚焦一个不同的主题：药物的其他形式、冥想、瑜伽、健康饮食等。这不是一档制作成本很高的系列节目，但是数百万人观看了它，而且报纸上有很多关于它的报道。

　　这是约翰的创意。他觉得人们对这个话题的关注度正在增长，但即便是他自己，也对观众的数量和报纸的关注度感到很惊讶。

● 第6页

　　"再跟我说说老板是怎么说的，约翰。"

"他说他认为这是他看过的……有史以来最好的系列节目。他还谈到报纸是多么喜欢这档节目。我们的总经理非常非常开心。他想和我聊聊钱的事，聊聊我的薪水，给我涨工资，难以置信吧？"

当他谈到薪水的时候，珍妮脸上的微笑消失了片刻。

"当然，也要给你涨工资！"约翰补充道。珍妮的笑容又回来了。"他认为这档节目可能会赢得蒙特勒金奖的最佳纪录片奖。"

"太棒了，"珍妮说，"我们做到了，我们成功了。我们真的做到了。"此刻珍妮独自在跳舞。

"当然成功了，"约翰开玩笑道，"我们相信它会成功，它就成功了。如果你坚信一件事情，它就一定会发生。它可能不会完全按照你想的方式发生，但是它一定会发生。如果我们相信某件事是真的，那它就会变成真的。这就是我们节目的意义所在。"

"你告诉雷切尔了吗？"珍妮问道，把他拉回到现实中来。

"我还没有机会给雷切尔打电话呢。我刚刚挂掉总经理的电话，还没来得及打。我现在就打。但是听着，我们午饭时再聊聊吧，我有一个关于另外一档节目的想法。"

● 第7页

雷切尔是约翰的妻子。他有什么好消息、坏消息或者没有消息，抑或是在心情低落或心情很好的时候，都会第一个跑去跟她倾诉。他们结婚接近两年了，在这段时间里，他们彼此间没有任何秘密。他们什么都对彼此讲。这就是他们的关系如此融洽、如此牢固的原因。他们聊彼此的感受、彼此的想法、彼此所做的事情，一切。他们之间没有秘密。

他拿起电话，还没等珍妮朝门口走就转过身背对着她，但是她并不介意。珍妮了解他，她知道他对妻子和儿子的爱，知道他有多么激动。她笑着离开了房间。她心想，每天都应该像这样。但是不行，那样每天就没有什么特别的了，而今天是一个特别的日子。

约翰坐在桌子旁边，手里拿着电话。他开心地环顾自己的办公室，然后望向窗外。从他五楼的办公室向外望去，这些风景在伦敦也是数一数二的：议会大厦位于西边，塔桥近得似乎触手可及，而整栋大楼则可以俯瞰泰晤士河。今天的河面上很热闹，有船只载着游客，还有一群办公室职员在一艘租来的游船上开生日派对。甚至巡河警察今天看上去也很放松，他们来回游弋在河面上，做着平时并不令人愉快的工作。

● 第8页

约翰几乎从不花时间向窗外看。他有时候会问自己，为什么电视公司要花那么多钱在伦敦这个美丽却又昂贵的地段租一栋大楼。在这栋大楼里工作的人们要么在外拍片子，要么在忙于各种会议，从不看向窗外欣赏风景。

或许有着这样风景的大楼只是为了给那些来买他们节目的英国和国外其他电视公司的访客看的。购买节目要花很大很大一笔钱，为了这些重要人士，你至少能为他们提供这样的风景。或许它可以帮助卖掉节目，特别是在像今天这样美丽的春日清晨。

此刻，约翰看着自己的办公室，想着自己节目的成功，自我感觉很棒。但随后他记起了手中的电话，记起他想跟雷切尔通话。他犹豫了一下，又把电话放下了。

● 第9页

约翰很担心雷切尔。她这几周似乎都不开心。她好像很紧张，在担心着什么事情。主要是担心他们年幼的儿子帕特里克。最近她哪里也不想去。在过去的两周里,他单独外出了至少三次,去聚会,去看戏剧,去和朋友聚餐。这些都是雷切尔喜欢的活动,但是她却不想出门,不想离开帕特里克。

有两次她半夜做噩梦后尖叫着醒来,从床上跳下来冲向帕特里克的房间。她抱起他,紧紧地把他搂在怀里。她的脸紧贴着他,一边哭一边颤抖,直到她的哭声慢慢地停下来,她才轻轻地把他放回床上。她没有回到他们的卧室,约翰于是起来去把她领回床上。

"怎么了?"他用胳膊搂着她问道,"怎么了,亲爱的,发生了什么?"他重复着。

"我不知道,我不知道。我只知道帕特里克发生了不好的事情。我不知道是什么。我在找他,但是到处都找不到他。我不知道,我不知道,我不知道怎么了。我只是害怕极了。"

● 第10页

她再一次哭起来,他又搂住她,直到她睡着了。起初,她在他的怀里扭动,甚至颤抖,后来她睡得安静些了,她的呼吸柔和地拂在他的脸颊上。

她醒来以后,不想提起那个梦,不想去回忆,所以他们就让这件事过去了。但是当天晚些时候,约翰发动汽车引擎时,她却抱着帕特里克从车上跑了下来。从那以后,她就拒绝乘车去任何地方。从那以后,如果她不得不去什么地方,她都抱着帕特里克走着去。每当有车经过时,她就停下来,双唇紧紧地抿成一条线,双手环抱着帕特里克,好像要保护他,好像她担心他会出什么事一样。

约翰心想,同时感到如此成功和如此担忧真是很奇怪。他再次拿起电话准备打给雷切尔,先前的兴奋感现在已经没了,他想知道自己的妻子正在努力保护帕特里克免受什么伤害。

第2章　生日快乐

● 第11页

"你没有忘记这周的生日吧。"雷切尔一在电话里听出他的声音就说道。

约翰没有立刻回答，不是因为他忘记了帕特里克的生日，更多的是因为她的声音让他感到惊喜和高兴。她的声音听起来很开心、很兴奋，并不焦虑。这是她原来的声音，她那甜美温柔的声音，对他来说就像是昔日的幽灵，一个非常受欢迎的幽灵。他放松双肩，长舒了一口气，对着电话微笑着。他差点儿就想说"欢迎回来"，但是他不愿提起过去这几周发生的事情。他怕这一刻会消失，怕一旦谈论起来，过去几周的担心和恐惧会重现。他转念说道："我们儿子的第一个生日，我怎么会忘记呢？你把我想成什么样的父亲了？"他用轻松、愉快的声音继续说："我只是不确定该为他的生日做些什么。我的意思是，这对他来说，对我们所有人来说，都是一个特别的日子，我只是想做些特别的事情……"。

● 第12页

他边说边想到了一个主意。当然，这会是一个完美的主意。

"我有一个主意。我们去爱尔兰度个短假吧。让我们再回到我们的地方，回到那个小岛。我想不出一个更好的地方来给帕特里克过生日了。"

"哇！你是认真的吗？我们可以去吗？你真能腾出时间来吗？我们什么时候去？"

他对她的问题报以朗声大笑。上一秒她还不相信他的话，下一秒她就在计划一切了。

"是的。是的。是的，我的老板很喜欢我。这个周末我们就去。"约翰依次回答了她的问题，又补充道："我现在就订票，等我到家后再告诉你为什么我的老板那么喜欢我。"

爱尔兰，西海岸附近的悬崖和小岛。他们一起去那里度过了他们的第一个假期。那个假期，他们在莫赫悬崖顶端一起跳舞。莫赫悬崖矗立在海面上，高一百多米。他在她的耳边哼唱，他们随着歌声起舞。雷切尔穿着一件浅白色的夏日连衣裙，他则修改了一首流行歌曲的歌词，对他的"白裙姑娘"唱着。

● 第13页

"爱尔兰会很冷。"他提醒过她。但是他很开心自己弄错了，他紧紧地抱着她，感受着她的温暖和温柔。就在那个假期，他们决定结婚，而假期结束不到九个月后，帕特里克就出生了。所以他们叫他帕特里克，一个爱尔兰名字。是的，爱尔兰对他们来说是个非常特殊的地方。

"你真的能抽出时间吗？"

"能，能，能。我告诉过你了，我的老板喜欢我。我现在要和珍妮去吃午饭了，然后我就回家，我们可以计划一下我们的旅行。"

"到那里以后，我们租一辆车，这样就可以开车到处逛逛了。"

一辆车，这是她的建议。过去的几个星期里她似乎很怕汽车，而现在她却建议租一辆车。约翰心想，她真的又是原来的那个她了，这让他非常高兴。

            *   *   *

午餐时，珍妮建议去圣保罗大教堂后面的一个意大利小餐厅。他们打车到了那里。他们依旧对节目的成功感到非常高兴和激动，像十几岁的孩子似的一路笑着闹着到了餐厅。

他们到那儿以后，点了一瓶餐厅里最好的红酒。食物上桌后，他们慢慢地品尝着，享受食物带来的快乐。他们不经常外出吃午饭。如果要吃些什么的话，他们通常都是在工作的地方吃个三明治。要是确实有时间外出吃午饭的话，他们通常会一边狼吞虎咽，一边滔滔不绝地交谈，完全不关注他们吃的是什么。

● 第14页

但是这次，他们直到饭后享用咖啡的时候才继续谈论工作的事。

"那么，你的新想法是什么？为什么不能等到明天再说？"珍妮吃完她那特浓的奶酪蛋糕，一边看着盘子确定没剩下任何东西，一边问道。

"也不是什么新点子。但是不管怎么样，我要先告诉你，我将休一周假去度个短假。所以你可以在我休息的时候工作！"

她朝他微笑着说道："你休息，我工作，的确没什么新意。那个想法是什么？"

"你还记得前段时间我们讨论过的那些都市传说吗？你知道的，就是那些在全国各地不同地方的人们讲述的故事。基本都是一样的故事，但是故事听起来就好像真的在那个地方发生过，就在那个城镇或者村庄。你懂我的意思吧？而没有人能确定那些故事是否真实。你还记得吗？"

● 第16页

"记得，就像那个在森林深处的汽车的故事。"她说。

"那是哪个故事？"约翰问道。

"你知道的，就是那个关于一对情侣深夜开车穿过森林回家的故事。他们的车没油了，男的去找油，女的待在车里。她等呀等，但是那个男的一直没有回来。"珍妮对自己讲的故事感到兴奋，开始压低嗓音，降低语速。"过了一会儿，那个女人听到从车顶传来一阵声响，就好像有人在敲车顶。她很害怕，便锁上了车门，然后一辆警车从后面开了过来。一个警察下了车并冲着她喊：'下车，朝我走过来，不要回头。'然后……"

"对，就是这类故事。"约翰微笑着说道，但是没有让她讲完。珍妮做了个鬼脸，好像对没能讲完这个故事感到失望。

"同样的故事，还有其他类似的故事在英国不同的城镇流传着，就好像是真的一样，但是从没有人发现过任何证据，也没有警方的记录或医院的记录，什么都没有。好吧，我的想法就是尽力再搜集一些这样的故事，找出它们的来源。我想看看人们是否一直在讲这样的故事，如果是的话，他们以前讲的是什么故事。或许我们可以用这些素材做一档节目。我不太清楚。你觉得怎么样？"

● 第17页

珍妮若有所思地点了点头。"或许可以，"她说，"这正好让我想起了前几天看到的一个关于神秘搭车人的故事。你知道类似的故事吗？"

约翰轻轻地摇了摇头，好像在思考着别的事情，好像他已经在度假了。

"好吧，你知道什么是搭车人，是不是？"珍妮开玩笑地问道。

"我当然知道，"约翰说，"我和雷切尔就是这样相识的！我们就是这样相遇的。"他微笑着回忆起来，珍妮意识到严肃的话题结束了，他想回家去找他的妻子和儿子了。

"好吧，我看看我能找到些什么。你休息的时候，我会做一些工作的。"

"我们就是这样相遇的。"约翰离开餐厅时这样想着。搭便车，他和雷切尔就是这样相遇的。

第 3 章　白衣女人

● 第18页

现在是周五上午，是约翰去爱尔兰度假前的最后一个工作日。约翰已经买了飞往爱尔兰的机票，预订了他们之前住过的那座乡间别墅，别墅位于离爱尔兰西海岸不远的一座小岛上。他还在都柏林机场预订了一辆车。一切准备就绪，他很期待这个假期，一心只想着这件事。电话响起的时候，他并没有在想工作的事情。

是珍妮。

"你还在这儿，是吗？"她问。

"哦是的，我还得在这里待一会儿。"

"我猜你不想谈工作了，是不是？"她问。

"好吧，说实话，不太想。"他说，"怎么了？你有什么事情要跟我说吗？"

"或许有。"

"或许有？"

"只不过是一些我觉得你可能会感兴趣的事情。"珍妮说，"我找到了一些关于都市传说的东西，就是那天午饭时我们讨论的事情。"

● 第19页

"真的吗？你一直没闲着啊！"

"是呀，我可没忙着做假期计划。"她笑着说。

"好啦，谢谢你的小玩笑。那你找到了些什么？"约翰问。

"嗯，我给不同的地方报社和广播电台打了电话，"珍妮解释道，"我猜想当地媒体更有可能报道这类故事。我给他们讲了我们那天说的几个例子，并让他们如果有什么发现的话，就给我打电话。我还在网上查了查，还去了中央图书馆，看能不能找到什么书。"

"那你找到什么了吗？"

"有一些有意思的报道，我还想进一步调查，此外……"她停了一下。电话中她沉默了很久。很显然她找到了一些有意思的事情，正在逗他，让他多等一会儿。这是他们之间的一个游戏。

约翰在电话里笑起来。他也喜欢玩这个游戏，所以他等了一会儿才问。

"此外你找到什么有意思的事情了吗？"

"找到了。"

"那就告诉我吧。"约翰说。

"你有时间吗？"

● 第20页

"珍妮！"他提高了嗓音，这说明他已经有点儿厌烦这个游戏了。

"好吧，好吧。但是别在电话里说了。"

"为什么不在电话里说？"他问道。

"因为我有东西想让你也听听。"

"好吧，但是现在就过来。我今天真的还有别的事情要做。行吗？"

不到两分钟，他办公室的门就开了，珍妮走了进来。

约翰又笑了。

"你真的是不浪费时间，对吧？"

珍妮也笑了，她把一个盒式磁带录音机放在了他面前的办公桌上。

"这是什么？"约翰问。

"我一会儿放给你听，但是先让我给你讲讲我是怎么找到这个的吧，好吗？"她说。

"好吧。"

"是这样的。这是我周二那天提到过的搭车人的故事。我从全国各地不同的地方报纸或者广播电台发现了三个关于搭车人的故事。我的意思是，真的是全国不同的地方。一个来自格拉斯哥，一个来自利物浦，一个来自剑桥郊外的小村庄。但是……"她又停顿了一下，再次让约翰等着，"……故事是完全一样的……完全一样。三个不同地方的三个不同的男人讲述着完全一样的故事。"

● 第21页

"或许他们彼此认识。"他说。

"我不这么认为。就像我说的，他们住在这个国家不同的地方，从事完全不同的工作，而且他们讲的故事发生在不同的年份。但是，总之，真正有意思的是，他们都说自己经历的这件事发生在完全相同的地点，就在布赖顿以北。"

"那么，他们为什么要去布赖顿呢？"他问，"我是说那是我周末离开伦敦时最喜欢去的地方之一，但是他们呢？"

"又是不一样的原因。一个人是去出差，另一个是送女儿回那里的大学，而第三个……"她看了看她的记录，"……去看了场足球赛。"

"那他们到底发生了什么事？"

"好吧，你自己听吧。"珍妮边说边从夹克口袋里拿出一盒磁带放进了录音机里。

"这是来自利物浦当地的一家广播电台的采访。他们和其中一个人聊了聊。我觉得他们没把这件事太当真，只是把它用作一档万圣节前夜节目的片段了。你知道的，都是有关鬼故事之类的内容。但是，当然了，电台那边并不知道另外两个人。不管怎么样，他们昨天把这个寄给了我。我认为你会觉得它很有意思的。"

● 第22页

"我们听听吧。"约翰一边说着一边自己按下了播放键。他想听听这个故事，但是他也想尽快摆脱工作，开始自己的假期。

磁带一开头没有声音，然后才开始播放。采访者先说话。

那么请给我们讲讲到底发生了什么吧。

嗯，我正开车从布赖顿往回返。我把我的女儿送去那儿了，送回大学。她二十二岁了，但是我妻子还是很担心她，所以我亲自开车把她送到了那儿。我正在回家的路上。路途很长，但是我喜欢开夜车，车少。那天天气很好，是一个晴朗而又干燥的夜晚。我刚刚开车穿过了一个小村庄，还开得很慢，然后，就在村外我看见了一个女人。她就站在路边……穿着一身白色的衣服，所以我一下子就看到了她。就在我开过她身边的时候，她伸出了手，好像要搭便车，然后我停下了。我是说，我一般不会停下来载搭车人，因为你永远不知道会载到什么样的人，对吧？但是，一个女人，在深夜，我想到了我的女儿，如果她在深夜独自外出的话，我知道我的感受会是如何，所以我停了下来。

● 第24页

然后呢?

她走到车后面。我打开车门,询问她要去哪里。"最近的汽车修理厂。"她说。于是我说:"上车吧。"她说:"谢谢。"她上了车,我继续开车。我看到她没有系安全带,就提醒了她一下,她看了看我,然后开始哭泣。她根本什么都没有说,就开始哭了。她一句话都没有讲,就开始哭了。我不知道是怎么回事。我问她:"你还好吧?"显然她并不好,她没有回答,只是继续哭。我不知道该怎么办,不知道该说些什么。我只是继续开车,不知道是否该停下或者……或者,做些什么其他的事情。我不知道。我刚决定要停车,这时她说道:"对不起,我……"她的呼吸仍然很急促,就好像在很努力地呼吸。但是她停止了哭泣。我还是吓得要命,头发都立了起来……我不知道该怎么办。

然后她说:"对不起,对不起。我们的车出了点问题,这就是我要去修理厂的原因。其他人都在车那里等着。我不知道自己为什么会那样哭起来。对不起。"我问我是否可以帮忙修车,问她车在哪儿,她说:"不用了,谢谢。修理厂会帮忙的。"她说车就在村外刚才我停下来载她的地方。不过,我不记得在村外的路上看到过有别的汽车停在那里,但我不想反驳她,你知道的。我不希望她又开始哭。她又沉默了,然后我注意到她在颤抖。"你冷吗?我可以把暖风打开。"她向我表示感谢,说是因为下雨,而且她浑身都湿透了。我转身看了她一会儿,注意到她的脸是湿的,她的头发和裙子也都是湿的。"这里下雨了吗?"我问道,因为那天我在任何地方都没有看到过一滴雨。

● 第25页

约翰把手放在录音机上，按下了一个按键。磁带停止了。

"他还没说完呢。"珍妮说道。

"你是从哪里弄到这个的？"约翰的声音很奇怪，冷冷的。

珍妮看着他。他脸上的表情很奇怪。珍妮从来没有见过约翰这样，也从未听过他用这样的语气说话。她突然觉得整个后背发凉。他的声音和表情让她感觉不舒服。比起磁带中的故事，这些更让她感到恐惧。

● 第26页

"我告诉过你，从利物浦，从当地的电台那里。"

约翰盯着那台录音机。他一动不动，脸变得苍白。

"怎么了，约翰？你还好吧？约翰？"

他似乎没有听到她说话，继续一动不动地坐了一会儿，然后才抬头看着她。

"这是怎么回事？这是什么玩笑吗？这是你开的玩笑吗？"

"不是啊。你是什么意思，玩笑？你在说什么？约翰，你在说些什么？这可不是玩笑。约翰，你吓到我了。你是什么意思？"

他看了她片刻，什么也没说，只是盯着她看，就好像想要把她看穿，看看她到底在想什么。然后他慢慢地点了点头，似乎是要表明他相信她不是在跟他开玩笑。

"或许他认识我。"

"谁？或许谁认识你？"

他看着录音机说："他，讲这个故事的男人。但是，他为什么要这么做呢？"

"做什么？你在说什么呢，约翰？"她担心地问道。这不是个玩笑，不是她开的玩笑，显然对他来说也不是玩笑。

● 第27页

"这是我的故事。"他轻轻地说，轻得她几乎听不到他在说什么。然后他稍微大声地重复了一遍："这是我的故事。"

"你的故事？怎么回事？我告诉过你，约翰，有三个人。他们都讲了同样的故事。这怎么会是你的故事呢？"

约翰再一次沉默了，坐在那里盯着办公桌。无法知道他的头脑里此刻在想些什么。他不停地摇着头，似乎在努力理解什么事情。

"这到底是怎么回事？我不明白。这是我的故事。他是怎么知道的？怎么知道的？我不明白。"

他们在办公桌两侧沉默着坐了一会儿。珍妮坐在那里看着约翰。她很担心，也有一点儿恐惧。她不知道该做些什么。她应该找人帮忙吗？离开他吗？跟他待在一起吗？说些什么吗？给他倒杯水吗？她该做些什么？她能做些什么……？

第 4 章　失控

● 第28页

珍妮还在试图决定做些什么，这时约翰突然伸手去够录音机并再一次按下了播放键。录音机里的声音继续讲述着故事。

……她说下了一整天的雨，或许那就是他们的车出故障的原因。然后她就不说话了，我害怕她可能又会哭起来，所以没有再说些什么。我没有再问任何问题。我只是开着车。那是个晴朗的晚上，我不明白这儿怎么会下雨，因为路面干得就像……我不知道怎么形容，但是真的非常干燥。

然后，过了一会儿，我觉得她又在看我。我努力不去理会，我不想看她。我的意思是她确实很漂亮。她上车的那一刻我就注意到了。真的很漂亮。深色的头发，澄澈的蓝眼睛。我打开车门的时候，从车里投射出的灯光让我看到了这一切。真的很美。正常情况下，我会在我们相互对望的时候感到很高兴。但是现在整个状况很奇怪，而且开始让我感到紧张。

● 第29页

然后我开始纳闷儿她为什么会因为一辆车而哭。我的意思是，我知道车出故障这件事很麻烦，特别是在深夜，但是它毕竟只是台机器，是不是？你还可以修好它……而且附近一定会有汽车修理厂的。所以我在想："她为什么为这事哭呢？"然后我又想："或许不是因为车，或许还发生了别的事情，或许她和一个男人什么的在一起，然后他……他做了什么事情……"于是我打算问她……看看她是否真的没事，我转过头看着她，她也在看着我。

她看着我……我很难描述那个眼神，但是……我不知道那是什么，好像她想要看透我是一个什么样的人。那是，我不知道，那眼神既性感又不确定，好像她不知道是否可以信任我。我的意思是，在眼泪和刚刚的一切过去之后，我感觉有一点儿兴奋和紧张，还有一点儿不自在。我是说，她比我的女儿大不了多少。

不管怎么样，我不喜欢她那样看着我，我移开了视线，重新看着路面。当我看到有路牌指示五百米处有一个汽车修理厂时，我感到很高兴。我只想快点儿让她下车。我说："我们很快就到那里了。"但是她没有回答。突然，正当我快开到一个拐弯处时，她开始尖叫。我的心一下子凉了，胃也猛地一紧，她在尖叫："天啊，我们要失控了，我们要失控了，当心，当心，天啊！"

● 第30页

我只是盯着路面……什么都没有，那儿什么都没有。路上空空荡荡的，汽车还像刚才一样行驶着。什么都没有，什么都没有发生。于是我转头去看她，就在这时，她突然把手放到了方向盘上开始拽……

约翰一直静静地坐在那里听着故事，一动不动，但是现在他突然在椅子上换了个姿势。他连连摇头，似乎他不同意某人的说法。

"不，不是那样的。不，不是那样的。不，她没有那样做，没有。"

珍妮坐在那里盯着他看。约翰在说什么？他是什么意思？她看到他又朝录音机靠近了一点儿，似乎想要听得更仔细，尽管那个男人继续用同样的方式讲述着，声音既没变大，也没变小。然后那个男人突然提高了声音，回想起那段往事时，他几乎是在大喊。

● 第31页

……我冲她大声喊："住手，住手！你在干什么？你想害死我们吗？"因为她拽着方向盘，车子左右摇晃，而我尽力让车在路面上直线行驶。她的力气很大，真的很大。我难以置信。她个子不高，身材很苗条。我不知道她哪里来的这么大的力气。真的很难对付。我用右手拼尽全力拉方向盘，同时用左手击打她的胳膊。

录音中男子停顿了一下，似乎他在为打一个女人这件事感到难为情，而且还是一个年轻女人，或许是一个像他女儿那么大的年轻女人。

然后呢？

汽车依旧在左右摇摆。我把脚放在刹车上，使劲踩着。但是由于她用力拽着方向盘，而我那样踩着刹车，车子就调转了方向。我失控了，真的失控了。我试图再次控制住车子，但是失败了。车撞到了路边的草地上，腾空而起，又落到草地上，然后停了下来。我就坐在那里，盯着马路，一动不动。我的手依旧放在方向盘上，紧紧地握着。然后，然后我长舒了一口气，就好像我一直在憋着气，而我的心跳得像火车一样。我能听见自己的心跳声，就像这声音是从我体外传出的一样。我握着方向盘的手都湿透了，我就坐在那里……然后，我想起了她。

● 第32页

"这到底是怎么回事？"我对着她大声喊道，"你为什么这么做？你到底怎么了？"但是她只是坐在那里，手捂着嘴，眼睛直直地盯着前方。后来她将脸上的乱发拨开，我看到她的脸上有什么东西。一些深色的东西从她的头发上顺着脸流了下来。我想那是血。于是我为自己对她大喊大叫而感到愧疚。我问她感觉怎样，但是可能我的声音依旧很大，她看着我，看起来很害怕。然后她的眼神从我的身上移开了，她试图打开门。起初她找不到把手，但是后来她找到了，成功地打开了门。

我还没来得及再说些什么，她就下了车沿着路往回跑了。我喊了几句。我不知道是什么。我不知道我喊的什么，接着我试图打开我这边的车门，但是我的安全带卡住了——一开始我怎么也解不开它，后来还是解开了。我打开车门，跳下车，追着她跑去。我跑到了马路的转弯处，仍继续跑着……然后……然后我停了下来。她不见了，消失了。路上什么都没有，一个人都没有，只有一条笔直而又空荡荡的马路。我的意思是，她穿着白色的衣服，你知道的。那是一个非常晴朗的夜晚，但是我看不到她。她没在那里。那里也没有别的路，没有别的岔口。路边什么都没有，只有两侧空旷的田地。她不可能就这样消失了。我站在那里，环顾着四周，这时一辆车沿着马路朝我开了过来。灯光弄得我眼花，司机边开过去边按着喇叭。他可能认为我喝醉了。我也觉得自己好像喝醉了。我感到很奇怪。

● 第33页

　　我走回到汽车那里，坐了一会儿，两眼发呆。但是之后又有两辆车开过转角处，司机冲着我按喇叭。这时我才意识到我的车正朝着相反的方向，我有点儿清醒过来了。我决定开车返回去，看看能发现什么。我开回刚才载她上车的那个村庄，但是那儿什么都没有。没有白衣女人，路边也没有停着里面有人等着的车子。什么都没有。我不知道该怎么办。报警吗？怎么说呢？说我在路边搭载了一名年轻女子，她哭了，然后她疯了，差点儿造成一起事故？说她凭空消失了？不能！我不能这么做……

● 第34页

　　但是我也不能继续开车了，而且也太晚了，找不到旅店或其他住的地方了。我决定停下来，在车里睡会儿觉，然后再继续开。但是我不想停在那个村子附近。我不知道为什么，但是我很害怕。我不知道该怎么想，但是我确定再也不想见到那个女人了。

　　是珍妮把录音机关掉了。她之前听过录音，知道这个男人已经讲完了。

房间里一片寂静。那个男人讲故事的时候，珍妮一直看着约翰。那个男人讲到那场事故的时候，约翰继续摇着头，低声说了几遍"不，不"。现在他就坐在那里，一动不动，一言不发，只是盯着录音机。珍妮感觉很不自在。录音机里播放着男人的故事时，她没觉得多糟糕，但是现在录音机里的声音停止以后，房间里只剩下她和约翰，她觉得很孤单。她想让他解释一下，但又很害怕。她从来没见过他这样。他坐在那里，沉浸在自己的世界里，她不敢再问他任何问题。

● 第35页

他们继续在那里坐了一会儿，然后约翰深深地吸了一口气，又吸了一口，然后抬头看着她。现在他的脸上非常平静。

"把你的车钥匙拿来，"他轻声说，"我来开车。带着你的手机，我们会需要它，还有那三个男人的电话号码，你都有吧？"

她点点头，很庆幸自己拿到了电话号码，也很高兴自己不必开口说话。她不知道是否能够控制住自己的声音。

"走吧。"他说着站起身来，快速朝门口走去。

她没有问他要去哪里。她依然不确定自己的声音是否稳定。她还有一种感觉，她已经知道他们要去什么地方了，但是她不太敢相信。

第 5 章 回忆之旅

● 第36页

他们开车穿过了滑铁卢桥，沿着繁华的主干道行驶到大象城堡区那个巨大的环岛。这个地方位于泰晤士河以南的伦敦地区，名字很奇怪，因为这里既没有大象，也没有城堡，只有许多脏兮兮的灰色办公楼，在一个很大的环岛中间有一个大型购物中心。

正是在环岛这里，珍妮看到了指向布赖顿的路标。"所以，我们就是去那里，"她想，"我们要去那些男人遇见搭车人的村子。"

她看了看约翰，但是他什么也没有说，只是继续注视着前方。

他们继续行驶着。珍妮看着窗外。城市的这个地区从来没有游客会来。这儿没有什么名胜，只有大片的房屋和公寓。每隔几公里就会看到路边有一些商店，这样的地方通常都叫作高街。这些街道看起来都一样，商店也都一样：博姿、W.H.史密斯、沃尔沃斯。你可以在伦敦的任何地区或英国的任何一个小镇找到完全相同的商店。

● 第37页

对珍妮来说这里同样没什么有趣的东西，但是她看着窗外的一切，就好像她一生中从没来过这里。观察沿途的一切，比去思考他们要做什么、要去哪里好得多，这样做也比试图猜测约翰在想些什么要好。

她和约翰在一起共事三年多了。他们很了解对方。她经常认为自己知道约翰在想些什么。她有时还能替他把话说完。但是现在，她不知道他在想什么。她也不确定自己是否想知道他在想什么。

他默默地开着车，甚至当突然有车蹿出来他必须要急踩刹车的时候，约翰都没有说一句话。这提醒了珍妮要系上安全带。她这样做时，想起了磁带里讲述的故事。那个人在故事中说了些关于安全带的事情。她努力回想那个人到底说了什么，但唯一浮现在她脑海里的，是从他们离开办公室时就一直困扰着她的那个问题。

● 第38页

约翰说"这是我的故事"时到底是什么意思？这个故事中到底有什么内容使她的老板脸色发白、沉默不语？她从来都不知道约翰可以沉默这么久。他通常都很健谈，只有在试图理解什么事情时才会安静下来。但即使那时什么也不说，他也会看着她。但是现在，他的脸上毫无表情，目光一直盯着车前方。珍妮又把自己的注意力转回到车外。

他们行驶在从克罗伊顿绕行至伦敦南部的路上，经过了曾经作为伦敦主要机场的旧机场。这里曾经是英国首相内维尔·张伯伦与希特勒在 1939—1945 年的大战爆发前开会后返回的地方。他走下飞机时手里挥舞着一张纸，一张希特勒签了字的纸。张伯伦把这份他和希特勒签署的协议称为"我们时代的和平"。珍妮的头脑中能闪现出那幅画面，尽管这是发生在她出生以前很久的事情。这一切发生的时候，甚至她的父亲也还很小。这是珍妮从别人那里听到的故事，但这不是她的故事，并没有直接触动她。这不是她的故事。

"这是我的故事。"约翰曾说过。

● 第39页

这句话在她的头脑中挥之不去。她的耳边依旧回响着约翰说这话时的声音，还有他脸上那难以置信的表情。她忘不了这一幕。他是什么意思呢？

当记者要写些什么东西而又不想让别的记者写时，他们有时候会说"这是我的故事"。但是约翰不是这个意思。他和珍妮一起合作撰写报道，他们之间没有竞争。那他是什么意思呢？

他们向南驶去时，城市渐渐被他们抛在了身后。他们驶过那些建在汽车飞驰而过的路边几米远的一排排小房子，那些房子有客厅，却没有可供孩子们玩耍的院子。有这么多车辆往来，这里对孩子们来说可不是个安全的地方。现在路过的是带有大庭院的大房子。接着他们来到了空旷的乡村，这儿没有什么车，有更多的路标指向布赖顿。他们离目的地越来越近了。

就在他们快要上高速公路的时候，她看到路边停着一辆车，一个男人正站在那里查看。他们没有减速就从他旁边驶过，她从侧后视镜里看着他。他正在查看发动机。他穿着讲究，她猜他应该不太了解发动机。想到自己曾经也有过类似的窘境，她不禁笑了。她对车也一无所知。她记得有一次坐男朋友的车，一起去一个森林公园漫步。她记得那是个美丽的地方。但是当他们回到车上想要启动发动机的时候，车却毫无反应。她的男朋友看了看发动机，尽管很快就找到了问题所在，但是他自己却修不了。

● 第40页

"我有一个主意，"他对她说，"你留在这里，无助地看着发动机，我去那边的咖啡店。正好我也想去上个厕所。"

珍妮当时不明白他说的是什么意思。但是不到两分钟就冒出一个男的，主动提出帮她并把车修好了。她想起这段经历忍不住又笑了。自那之后她就没怎么见过那个男朋友了，而且她总是买自己可以买得起的最好的车。她不想大半夜在某个荒无人烟的地方车子就抛锚了，不想像那个白衣女人一样，夜里在空荡荡的路上搭便车。

珍妮想起了另外一些事情，她脸上的笑容消失了，那是约翰在那家意大利餐厅说的话，关于雷切尔的，是他们谈论搭便车时约翰说的。是的，现在她记起他说的话了。他说："我和雷切尔就是这样相识的。搭便车。我们就是这样相遇的。"

● 第41页

　　珍妮顿时感到心里发凉。"这是我的故事。"约翰的话再一次回响起来，慢慢地，一个新的问题在珍妮的脑海中浮现。有没有可能约翰和雷切尔相遇的方式与录音中那个人描述的一样？

　　"那不可能。"

　　她意识到自己大声说出了这句话，而不是只在脑海中静静地想。她紧张地看向约翰，但是他继续盯着前方，就好像什么也没有听见。她很庆幸他没有听见。她不想告诉他自己在想什么。她自己也不确定自己在想些什么。同样的话在她的脑海中不断重复，一遍又一遍。"那不可能。那不可能。"

　　在她听到磁带中的声音，以及另外两个男人的故事时，她在想什么呢？是在想这是一个很有趣的例子，同样的故事是如何在全国各地从一个地方传到另一个地方，而且是用完全相同的方式被叙述的，就好像是真的一样，就好像确实发生过一样？她是否有那么一刻想过这故事本身含有某种真实成分？是什么呢？那个女人是鬼吗？

● 第42页

　　"那不可能。"

　　再一次，她不确定自己是说出了这句话还是只在脑子里想了想，或者约翰的确说了这句话。她转头看着他。他正慢慢地摇着头，好像也在思考："那不可能。"约翰真的说了这句话吗？约翰想的和她想的一样吗？

　　但是她没有时间再去多想了。在路边，她看到了下一个村子的名字。她从那些男人的故事中认出了这个村子的名字。他们正抵达那三个男人遇见搭车人的村子。

约翰开车进入村子时，她一动不动地坐着。他没有减速继续往前开，突然一个新的问题闪现在她的脑海中。录音中的男人没有提过村子的名字！她是从当地电台的记者那里知道的。录音中的男人没有提到村庄的名字，而她也没有告诉约翰。

● 第43页

"或许我们不是要在这里停下，"她想，"或许我们要去别的地方。或许这和约翰的故事不一样。"当这些想法充斥着她的大脑时，约翰看了看车子的后视镜，减速并把车掉了个头。他把车开回去穿过村子，正好停在村外，在马路对面，珍妮之前就是在那里看到了村子的名字。

然后，约翰开口和她说话了，这是他们离开办公室以后他第一次说话。他的声音平静而沉稳。

"这里就是我第一次见到雷切尔的地方，这里就是我第一次见到我妻子的地方。她要搭便车。她就站在那里。我正开车回伦敦。我停下了车。她就站在那里。我让她上了车。她穿着一条裙子。她穿着一条白色的裙子。她就站在那里……"

(第 6 章　警察的讲述——事故)

● 第44页

珍妮正在打电话。她站在距离约翰几米远的地方，他看着她，听着她说话。这是他的主意，让给遇到搭车人的三个男人中的一个打电话。这就是为什么在离开办公室的时候他告诉她要带上手机和电话号码。她正在跟其中一个人通话。她已经试了另一个号码，但是没有人接。拨了第二个号码后，电话几乎立刻就接通了，那个人很高兴接到她的电话。

约翰只能听到珍妮这边的对话。

"是的，我们就在村外。"

"是的，向北朝向伦敦。"

珍妮转过身看了看身后的什么东西。

● 第45页

"是的，我可以看到。"

"是的。"

"好的，谢谢您的帮助。"

"是的，如果我们决定制作这个节目，我会给您打电话的。"

"谢谢。好的，再见。不，我想那没必要了。再见。"

珍妮把电话放回到口袋里。

她和约翰站在那里互相看了对方一小会儿。"所以这里就是他遇见那个搭车人的地方？"约翰问道。

"是的。就是这里。"

"他确定？"约翰问。

"他说他永远也不会忘记这个地方。是的，就是同一个地方。"珍妮回答道。

"我也是在同样的地方遇见的雷切尔。"

珍妮不知道该说些什么。这到底是什么意思呢？约翰和雷切尔相遇的地方和那三个男人遇到神秘搭车人的地方是一样的，这意味着什么呢？

他们继续互相看着对方，一言不发。他们俩都不知道要说什么，似乎也不知道现在该做什么。最后，珍妮打破了沉默。

● 第46页

"我要给警方打个电话。"她说。

"为什么?"

珍妮没有回答约翰。她自己也不知道为什么要给警方打电话。她只是觉得她应该做些什么。她不想只和约翰沉默地干站在那里,他沉浸在他的想法里,而她沉浸在她的想法里。珍妮每次遇到窘迫的情况都会做些什么。她讨厌让人不舒服的沉默。行动起来,做些什么总能让她感觉好些。通常她做的事情就是逃离,能跑多快跑多快。她像这样甩掉了很多男朋友。但是尽管她在这儿感觉不舒服,但这是她的工作——她不能丢下约翰不管。

她打电话给接线员,得到了布赖顿警察局的电话。布赖顿警方建议她向几公里外的一个村子里的当地警方了解情况。他们告诉了她怎么去那里。

* * *

尽管村子不大,但他们还是花了很长时间才找到警察局。警察局是一座很普通的房子,有自己的院子。一辆车停在外面,是蓝色的,很干净,车里面没有什么东西,没有磁带,没有杂志,没有废纸。看起来不像是家庭用车,但也不像是通常带有鲜亮红蓝标志的白色警车。车身上只在车身侧面用小字写着"警察",其他地方都没有。前门旁边墙上的"警察"标志也很小。

● 第47页

很难相信这竟然真的是一个警察局。但是当门打开的时候,一个穿着深蓝色警服的警察站在门口。他是个中年人,大约五十多岁。他冲着他们微笑。珍妮觉得应该没有很多人来这里找他——这里看上去不像是一个忙碌的警察局。警察邀请他们先进了一间小办公室,然后又进了它旁边的接待室。

"在这里待着会更舒服些。"他说。

他们还没来得及解释为什么来这里，那个警察就提出要给他们泡杯茶时，珍妮并没有感到惊讶。她接受了。她一个人在说话，约翰坐着一言不发。这不像是平时的约翰，那个喜欢领导别人、喜欢掌控一切的约翰。珍妮再一次回忆起磁带里的话："我们失控了。我们失控了。"有那么一刻，她想知道约翰是否也失控了。她从没有见过约翰这样。她从没有见他如此安静，什么也不说，几乎一动不动。

● 第48页

警察去厨房的时候，珍妮环顾了一下他的房间。房间也非常整洁。这是一个独居多年的人的房间，仅有几件个人物品，而且摆放得井井有条。角落里有个书柜，里面的书都摆放得非常整齐。没有书是平着放的，书与书之间没有空隙，所有的书都竖直放着。有那么一刻，珍妮想知道那些是不是真的书，但是她没有过去查看。

她转而看向电视机旁边的小桌子上的三张照片。都是黑白照片，其中两张照片里是年轻的夫妇，不是同一对夫妇，但他们都看着摄影师，微笑着。其中一张照片中的夫妇穿着正式，看起来好像是专业摄影师拍摄的。从他们的穿着来看，照片大概拍摄于 20 世纪 30 年代。

珍妮觉得第二对夫妇的照片要照得晚些，看起来也更自然。照片中的这对夫妇正在某个地方度假，身后是大海。第三张照片是一个非常小的男孩儿，大概只有一岁吧。珍妮看着照片，猜想这些人和这个警察之间的关系。那对老夫妇会是他的父母吗？另一对夫妇是他和他的妻子吗？现在她在哪里？这个小男孩儿是这个警察的儿子吗？这里再没有别的照片了。

● 第49页

她想知道他的故事是否幸福。她希望是幸福的。警察端来茶时，她看向约翰。她想，约翰正看着那个小男孩儿的照片。这个男孩儿可能和帕特里克一样大。是的，她希望这是个幸福的故事。

● 第50页

* * *

当珍妮向那个警察解释他们为什么来这里，并跟他说了神秘搭车人的故事时，他看起来若有所思。

"你听说过附近发生过这样的故事吗？"珍妮问他。

警察笑了笑。

"好吧，我不能说我听过。这周围很僻静，很少有什么事情发生，所以如果有什么事情发生的话，每个人都会谈论它，你知道我的意思吧。"他轻声笑了笑。"这是个安静的地方。如果有什么事发生的话，人们喜欢谈论它，喜欢八卦。所以，我确定没有听过任何鬼故事。"

珍妮觉得他快速地瞥了瞥那张年轻夫妇在海边的照片，但是她对他刚才说的话更感兴趣。"鬼。"她和约翰都没有提过这个词。自从约翰听了磁带里的故事，自从约翰说了"这是我的故事"之后，她不想提起这个词，当然也不想说。

警察继续聊着，约翰看着珍妮。

"你说他们在村子附近遇见了这个女人？这三个男人都是在同样的地方遇见的她吗？"

"是四个。"

● 第51页

警察看着约翰，约翰重复道："四个，四个男人都遇见了她。"

"对不起，我以为你刚才说的是三个人报告了同样的事情。"警察再次看向珍妮说。这是他第一次听起来有些正式，更像是一个正常的警察。

"或许是四个。"珍妮说，然后很快继续说了下去。

"但是，是的，是在同一个地方，就在村子的北面，实际上就在村子的指示牌附近。"

"你是说在指示牌附近吗?"他想了一会儿，他的表情表明他在非常努力地回忆着。然后开心的笑容再次出现在他的脸上——他想起来了。

"是的，有件事情，的确有件事情，我刚才忘了。"

他刚才努力回忆时一直看着天花板。现在他的眼神又回来了，他看着珍妮，笑容完全消失了。

"是一起事故，"他边说边看向地板，"一起很严重的事故。"他看起来好像不想再多说什么，似乎回想起这件事又勾起了他极其痛苦的情绪。

他站起身来，朝着办公室走去，几分钟后当他回来的时候，手里拿着一些文件。他坐下来开始说话，但没有触碰放在他膝盖上的文件。

● 第52页

"这起事故是起 SCA。"他的语气再一次变得更为正式。"我们是这样命名的，SCA，一辆车出的事故。仅有一辆车，然后就发生了事故。有时候是司机喝醉了。有时候甚至可能是有人想要自杀，自杀。"

说这话时，他抬头看了看珍妮，然后很快补充道："对不起，女士，我不是说这起事故是这样发生的。我确定这起事故与喝酒或者……或者和自杀都没有关系。就是有时候……"

他没有把话说完。他似乎很担心珍妮，就好像他是在和交通事故中遇难者的家属说话，而不是和电视台记者说话一样。珍妮点了点头，冲着警察微微一笑。她一般不喜欢别人称呼她"女士"。她当然不喜欢别人因为她是女性而对她区别对待。但是她无法对这位友好的警察生气，因为他在回忆这起事故时，自己看起来也很伤心。

"继续吧。"她轻声说道。

"司机似乎在村外的转弯处失控了。或许她开得太快了，或许车里发生了什么事情。我们不知道。后来我们检查了车辆，发现刹车和方向盘都没有任何异样。但在这样一起事故中，很难讲是怎么回事。"

● 第53页

他看着他们。

"你们真的想知道更多关于这件事的细节吗？"他问道。

珍妮点了点头。警察继续说起来。

"那是一个下大雨的夜晚。"

警察讲到这里时，约翰在椅子上向前坐了坐。这是他从进到警察的这间接待室以来第一次挪动身体，第一次表现出他在听，表现出他很感兴趣。

"地面很湿，"警察继续说，"汽车偏离了马路，撞向了一棵树，就是这样。他们……他们俩当场死亡。"

"他们？"约翰和珍妮同时问道。

"那个女人……和……和孩子。村里的人们听到了撞车的声响都跑了出来。附近住着一位医生，但是……但是他也无能为力，什么都做不了。他们都死了。"

● 第54页

"那个男孩儿多大了？"约翰看着警察桌上的照片问道。

警察对这个问题很震惊。

"我没有说那是个男孩儿啊。你是怎么知道的？"

约翰什么也没有说，但是在警察回答约翰问题的时候，珍妮感觉自己的心沉了一下。

"只是个婴儿，甚至还不到一岁。"

"就像我的儿子帕特里克一样，"约翰说，"就像帕特里克一样。"

第 7 章　约翰的故事

● 第55页

警察继续讲述着。他没有看自己膝盖上的文件，只是茫然直视着，似乎这样可以帮助他回忆。他平静地讲述着，没有停顿。

"我们试图联系她的家人，但是我们没有找到任何人。在她的驾照上有一个伦敦的地址。伦敦的警察去了那里，他们跟周围的邻居聊了聊。邻居说她在那里只住了几个月，自己一个人。我的意思是，她和孩子独自生活。他们说她很安静，但很少外出。

"她在外面遇到邻居时总是很友好，但是她很少谈论自己的事情。她显然很爱她的孩子。她似乎很幸福。邻居们没有看到任何访客来过她家。他们很奇怪她的身边没有男人。你知道人们总是这样。他们看到一个女人带着一个小孩儿，就会好奇为什么身边没有男人。但是，他们确实没有看到任何男人或其他访客，除了事故前的那个星期。

● 第56页

　　"邻居们说一个年轻的女人一周前来这里留宿过，她们俩看起来长得很像。邻居们认为她们可能是姐妹。他们说另一个女人看起来好像是从热带国家来的。她的皮肤很黑，被太阳晒黑的。警察在公寓里找到了一个打包了一半的行李箱。他们不知道这个行李箱是谁的。上面没有地址，什么都没有。他们甚至无法判断这是个打包了一半还是拆开了一半的行李，是有人刚刚到这里，还是有人要离开。

　　"他们到伦敦登记处查证，找到了这位女士和她的姐妹的出生日期。他们还查到了她们父母的死亡记录。但这就是他们查到的全部了。税务局那边有这位女士的记录，但是没有她的姐妹的。记录显示她在一家电脑公司工作了两年，然后离开了。公司对她后来的情况一无所知。就是这样了。这就是我们查到的所有信息。一辆车出的事故，一个女人和她的孩子死了。没找到家人。真悲惨，非常悲惨。"

　　他们沉默了许久。警察讲完故事后，看着地板。然后转过身再次看了看那些照片。他在椅子上挪动的时候，文件从他的膝盖上掉了下来，响声似乎把他从回忆中拉回到了现实。他弯腰去捡文件。当看到其中一页上的某个东西时，他停了下来。他点了点头，轻轻地说，就像是自言自语。

● 第57页

　　"当然，另一个女人。"

　　他抬头看着他们，一边回忆一边依旧点着头。

　　"还有件事情，奇怪的事情。有些村民记得在汽车旁边看到了一个年轻的女人。她是个陌生人。我的意思是没有人认识她，她不是这个村子的人。她站在离汽车几米远的地方。她没有看着汽车，只是站在那里，把手包紧紧贴在胸前，一直哭。其中一个村民用一只手臂抱住她，想要让她感觉好一些。他不知道事故之前她是否也在这辆车里，或许她是从另一辆看到事故而停下来的车里下来的。"

那个警察停顿了一下，试图回忆起更多，当他想不起来时，他翻看了一会儿文件。他对自己没有想起来似乎有点儿失望。然后他继续说起来。

● 第58页

"救护车很快就到了，那个村民跟着一起帮忙。他告诉救护人员还有一个女人。他觉得他们应该看看她，确认一下她没事。但是他们没有找到她。他们找过她，但没有找到。"

他又看了看文件，然后读道："一个穿着白色衣服的年轻女人也出现在了事故现场，但是在警方到达现场来询问事故情况之前她就离开了。"

*　*　*

珍妮开车离开了警察局，约翰则坐在副驾驶座位上。他们驶回到事故发生的那个村庄。他们路过之前停留的地方，就是雷切尔搭约翰便车的地方。他们俩都没有说话。他们继续行驶着，几分钟后，来到了一个加油站。

"在这里停一下。"约翰说。

珍妮把车停在加油站后面。车还没有停稳，约翰就开始说话了，而且说得很快。

"那天晚上我就是在这里放下雷切尔的。我在这里放下了雷切尔，这和那几个人的故事不一样。这里不同。我让她搭了便车，她全身湿透了，穿着一条白色的裙子。我们聊了相同的关于汽车的话，和录音中那个男人说的一样。她的确开始哭泣。这些都一样。她确实像录音中那个男人描述的那样看着我。但是我看着她，我们都笑了。我们冲着对方微笑，然后来到了这里，我停了车。"

● 第59页

所以，这就是约翰所说的"这是我的故事"的意思，珍妮想。在某种意义上，珍妮对他刚刚告诉她的这些并不感到惊讶了。

"她没有喊些什么吗？她没有把手放在方向盘上吗？"

"没有，没有。没有那样的事情。我在这里和她分开了。我再一次问她是否确定我真帮不上什么忙。她说'是的'，她又说'谢谢'，微笑着，下了车。但是她没有立刻关上车门。她似乎在等待什么。而我只是问她，或许，我是否还可以再见到她。我说我想找个时间给她打电话来确定……"

约翰回忆起这些时笑了。这是很长时间以来珍妮第一次看到他笑。她伸出手，碰了一下他的胳膊。

"我想要再见到她。"约翰说。

● 第60页

"你做到了，你的确又见到了她，并且……"珍妮停了下来。她不知道怎么继续。

约翰用手捂住脸。珍妮不知道他是否在哭泣，但是当他再次开始说话时，他的声音已经哽咽。

"这到底是怎么回事，珍妮？这些到底与我有什么关系，与雷切尔有什么关系？这一切意味着什么？我不知道这是怎么回事。太疯狂了。我不相信这些。我不……我不知道该相信什么。"

"你想要这些意味着什么，看在上帝的分上？"珍妮几乎是在对他喊。她不是生他的气，但是这样对着他大喊让她在说出自己的话时更有勇气。

"你在路上遇见了雷切尔，她说她的车子出了问题。你让她搭车来到了加油站。你觉得她很漂亮。她确实很漂亮。你想再见到她。你约她出来。你确实又见到了她。你们相爱了。你……你知道后来发生的事情了。你还想要怎么样？为什么你还要有别的想法？"

"那这些男人的故事呢？"他说。

"他们的故事和你的相似，的确，但还是有不同的地方。你自己刚才也说了。是有不同的地方啊。我知道这很不寻常，这很奇怪，但也仅此而已。这件事非常不寻常，但是这并不意味着什么啊。他们的故事和你没有关系。"

● 第61页

"那他们的故事是怎么回事？"约翰问，"你觉得他们身上发生了什么？你觉得他们提到的白衣女人是谁？你怎么以你记者的眼光来看这个事情？"

珍妮停了一下，但只是一会儿。她喜欢当记者。

"那个女人，你知道的，就是事故现场的那个女人，可能是那个姐妹，汽车里那个女人的姐妹。或许她也在车里。或许因为车祸她失忆了。事故中的人有时是会这样的。他们不知道自己在哪里，或者自己是谁。有时候，他们会失忆很久。所以这个女人也是受了惊吓。她走进夜色中。我不知道她要去哪里，她也不知道自己要去哪里。她只是走着离开了，去了某个地方。或许有人让她搭了便车。或许有人找到她并帮助了她，但她什么都不记得了。后来，她想起了这个地方。她想不起别的事情，但是她记得这个地方，所以她回来了。她希望她能回忆起一切。这种事确实会发生。事故中的人撞到了头，失去了记忆。没有人在找她。她唯一的亲人在事故中去世了，所以没有人报告她的失踪。这种事确实会发生。"

● 第62页

珍妮的声音现在越来越激动，再次被自己讲述的故事所吸引。

"不管怎么样，她回来了，她回到了这个地方。她记得这个地方，记得在这附近搭了车。她想记起其余的事情。这就是她回到这里的原因。她不知道自己是谁，自己失去了什么，她不知道自己身上发生了什么事情。她什么都不知道。她寻找的不仅仅是记忆，那里可能有人在等她，在找她，她不知道。她希望也许回到这里，再搭一次便车，能帮她回忆起一切。所以她尝试着，一次又一次地尝试。"

"直到她遇见了我？"

"你能不能别再想这个了？我们不是在谈论雷切尔！"珍妮现在几乎是在对着约翰大叫。"这是不同的人。事实上，你在这里遇见雷切尔只是个巧合！汽车确实会抛锚，你知道的，而且下雨的时候女人是会淋湿的。你也非常清楚这里可能下雨而路面会完全干燥。这里是英国，不是撒哈拉沙漠！"

● 第63页

她现在生他的气了，但是她不确定是为什么。或许是因为她很害怕，害怕约翰不相信她，害怕她自己也不知道是否应该相信这个故事。

"那个白衣女人总是会消失？"

"她没有消失，约翰！她只是从自己差点儿引发的事故现场逃走了。她很害怕，不记得自己的过去了。她只记得自己一次又一次来到这里，同样的事情一遍遍发生，就好像不由她控制。她感到害怕，然后就逃走了，藏在田野里，或者其他什么地方，或者任何可以藏身的地方。她不想向司机解释这一切。"

珍妮靠在汽车座椅上，被自己讲的故事弄得筋疲力尽。然而，她想，她的故事可能是真的。她想相信这一点。她的故事是真实的这个想法让她平静了一些，也让约翰平静了一些。他坐在她的旁边，点着头。

"还有什么别的事情是你想相信的?"珍妮直面自己难以置信和无法言明的恐惧继续道，"雷切尔是鬼? 回家，用手臂搂着她……还有帕特里克。如果雷切尔是鬼的话，那帕特里克是什么呢? 那太疯狂了，约翰，那太疯狂了。回家吧，把她抱在怀里，然后打电话告诉我她是个鬼。好吗?"

● 第64页

她大笑起来，尽管那笑声并不是十分自然。她看着约翰，她觉得，她希望，自己看到了约翰眼中开始出现一丝笑容。

"回家去找你的家人。去爱尔兰度假吧。远离工作。忘记这个故事。你最近工作太辛苦了，太长时间没有休假了。离开这里，直到你把这一切都忘了再回来。"

第 8 章　爱尔兰——平和与回忆

● 第65页

船离开了爱尔兰的小渔港，来到了开阔的大西洋，朝着伊尼什博芬岛驶去。天气很好，是一个温暖的晴天，几乎没有风。海水的起伏温和而缓慢，就像在进行长而慢的呼吸。雷切尔抱着帕特里克站在船尾。帕特里克盯着那些跟着船飞翔的鸟，有时候它们飞得离船很近，帕特里克几乎可以触碰到它们，他笑着，很开心，为他的生日礼物感到很兴奋。约翰希望这个假期是给他们全家最好的礼物。

这只是他们在爱尔兰的第二天，距离他和珍妮去布赖顿的那趟行程仅三天。约翰努力忘记去布赖顿的事情，努力忘记录音中那个男人提到的故事和警察所讲的故事。他没有跟雷切尔提起任何关于他最后那天上班的事情。那些故事使他感到恐惧。那个男人讲的故事与他和雷切尔初次相见的情形那么相似，这使他感到恐惧。他不想和雷切尔谈论这件事。他不知道怎么告诉她，也不知道该告诉她什么。不管怎么样，告诉她会让这一切显得真实无比。他宁愿把它当作一个梦，一个他可以忘记的梦。

● 第66页

他希望在爱尔兰度假会让他感觉好一些，会帮助他忘却烦恼。这是一个他自己曾多次来度假的地方，也是他和雷切尔第一次一起来度假的地方。在这里他总是能够平静下来。他希望那些平静的感觉现在会再次回来。现在，他比以往任何时候都更需要那种平静的感觉。

他站在船头，注视着矗立在他们刚刚离开的渔港后面的康纳马拉地区七座黑黑的圆形的山。它们不是很大的山，达不到世界级水平，但是从海平面上看还是够高的。它们看起来也非常迷人，很有吸引力，很有安全感。但是如果天气变了的话，这儿的天气变化得很快，如果大西洋上有雾和雨飘来的话，那里就会变得很危险。当你在浓雾中看不到自己面前的脚时，那里也会变得非常危险。你会迷失方向，然后可能就永远消失了。

船在莫赫悬崖旁边转弯了，黑色的悬崖从大海中拔地而起，高达一百多米。约翰仰望着悬崖，觉得自己很渺小。他只能隐约看见悬崖顶部有些微小的影子，难以置信那竟然是人。他们看起来那么渺小，那么遥远。

● 第67页

他和雷切尔第一次来度假时就沿着这些悬崖走过。他们在日落时独自来到这里，伴随着耳边他唱的歌曲，他们跳着舞。然后他们又走远了一些，直到他们停下来，静静地站在那里。他们俩站在悬崖边上的一个小墓碑前，沉浸在自己的思绪中，默默无语。他们弯下腰，读着上面写的字：

<blockquote>
致肖恩

我们每日都在思念你。

我们期待着与你再次在一个美好的地方重逢的那一天。
</blockquote>

墓碑上面没有日期，没有写明肖恩是怎么或是在什么时候去世的。没有写明他的年龄，也没有写明是谁为了纪念他而在距离悬崖边缘仅一米的地方立了这块墓碑。

约翰靠近悬崖边缘想俯瞰深邃的蓝绿色海水掀起的海浪，但是雷切尔猛地抓住他的胳膊，把他拉了回来。

"约翰，别这样。小心点。"

他朝她笑了笑。

● 第69页

"没关系的。"

然后他弯下腰，捡起一块小石头，从悬崖边轻轻地扔了出去。他努力想看着石头坠入大海，但是石头在距离水面还很远时就消失在了他的视线中，在它坠入海里永远消失在海洋中时，他也没有听到任何事声音。

船上人们的欢呼声让约翰从回忆中清醒过来。他四下看了看，不知道发生了什么。每个人都在欢呼着。他寻找着雷切尔和帕特里克，但是他们不在原来的地方了。就在他盯着船后的大海看的时候，一种突如其来的恶心感从他的胃中涌了上来。

他觉得自己能在水中看到些什么。但是欢呼声是从船的侧面传来的，当他从楼梯上跑下来的时候，他看到几乎船上所有的人都在这里。他看到了雷切尔和帕特里克在船的侧面附近。帕特里克正在指着什么，大声喊叫着。他的眼睛和嘴巴都张得很大。约翰看了看船的侧面，但是什么也没有看到。

但是接着，突然间，一个黑灰色的东西从水中跳了出来又潜了下去，跳出来又潜进去，一次又一次，他意识到那是一只海豚，海豚正在船的侧面游着，与船竞速。

● 第70页

又一只海豚出现了，两只海豚现在一起从水中跃起，然后又潜回冰冷的海水中。

"看啊，帕特里克，"他走到雷切尔的身后时听到她说，"海豚妈妈来了，来确保它没事。它照看着它，就像我照看着你一样。看到了吗？"

小一点儿的海豚又跟着他们游了一段距离，但是大一点儿的海豚没有再出现，然后小的那只也从船的侧面游走了，最后还跳了一次，好像是在说再见。

"好兆头。"一个站在约翰旁边的男人说道。约翰不确定这个人在对谁说话。"他们照看着在海上航行的人们，那些处于危险之中的人们。这也是生命的象征，你知道的，甚至是死后生命的象征。"那个男人说道。

"真的吗?"约翰问道，但是帕特里克此刻在他的耳边吵闹着关于那条"鱼"的事情，约翰只好转过身听帕特里克说话。

当船到达伊尼什博芬岛的时候，他又看到了那个男人，但是只是在那个男人离开港口的时候远远地望见了。约翰和雷切尔等着所有人都下了船。然后收拾了一下装满食物和衣服的行李，他们也下了船。到那个时候，那个男人已经不见了，当他们走向小别墅时，也没有再看见他。

● 第71页

小别墅位于岛的东海岸，多数的海岛居民住在这里。这里仅有十或十二座别墅，都朝着爱尔兰大陆的方向。这里还有两个酒吧，人们晚上会来这里听音乐，喝健力士黑啤。

＊　＊　＊

约翰特别喜爱西海岸，那里荒凉而空旷，没有人居住，来自北大西洋的风呼啸而过。

"下一站，纽约。"约翰站在那里，望着空荡荡的大海自言自语道。在岛上一周的假期已经接近尾声了，他最后一次独自出来散步，从岛的一端走到另一端。从悬崖高高伫立、无法到达海岸的北端，走到更加温和的南端，那里绵羊吃着草，把草地啃得矮小、平整，就像高尔夫球场上的草一样。

他喜爱这个地方。他现在已经走了快三个小时，看到成百上千的鸟儿随风飞翔，潜入海中捕鱼。他还看到数百只绵羊，在他靠近前就惊恐地叫着跑开了。这一路上他没有看到一个人。准确地说，他曾俯瞰过一个金色的小海滩，看到两辆自行车倒在沙滩上，还有两行朝着悬崖底部延伸而去的脚印，似乎是一对年轻的恋人正在寻找一处僻静的地方。

● 第72页

但是他没有看到任何人。这就是为什么他现在停下来，看着坐在海边岩石上的那个穿黑衣服的人。约翰距离那个人可能有二百多米远，所以很难看清楚那是个男人还是女人。那个人穿着黑色套装，留着非常短的头发，或者说根本没有头发，但是从这个距离看，约翰只能看到这些。他，如果是个男人的话，一动不动地坐在那里，望着大海，连头也不转一下，完全不动。约翰站着看着那个人，然后他也转身朝着大海，朝那个人看的方向看去。他什么也没看到，当他转过身来的时候，那个人不见了，消失了。但这没有什么可奇怪的。这里有很多地方他可以去，岩石遮挡住了视线。或许那个人注意到了约翰，便决定去找一个可以完全独处的地方。约翰能理解这一点。他也在寻找同样的地方。他只是希望那个人不要靠近那个水池，那个属于他的水池。

● 第73页

那个水池是一个岩石水池，就在海边几米远处。每天海水拍打岩石的时候，它被海水一次又一次填满。约翰之前独自来到小岛时发现了这里。当来到水池边的时候，他已经走了好几个小时了，双脚又热又累。他在水池边的一块岩石上坐了下来。

起初，他只脱下了鞋子和袜子，把脚放在凉爽平静的水中。池水非常凉爽，令人神往。然后约翰环顾四周，确定周围没有人后，便脱下了所有的衣服，慢慢爬进了水池中。他没怎么游泳，因为水池很小。相反，他只是仰面躺在水中，看着几小朵白云在广阔的天空中疾驰。

然后他整个身体翻过来面朝下待了一会儿，他睁着眼睛，闭着嘴巴，胳膊在身体下方耷拉着，一动不动，几乎像是死了一样。当这个想法出现在约翰的脑海中时，他在水中翻了个身，害怕有人从这里路过，看到他，以为他死了。

现在他又来到了水池边。他脱掉衣服，爬进水池，就像第一次做的那样。然后，像以前一样，他用棉衬衣擦干身体，躺在水池旁边的草地上睡着了。但是这次他的睡眠不会那么安宁了。

第 9 章　在水池边入睡

● 第75页

他在小别墅里醒来，尽管一开始他并不知道自己在哪里。他静静地躺了一会儿。周围很黑，他看不大清东西。他只是凭借着气味才知道自己在哪里，那是在爱尔兰西部他们在壁炉里烧过的干燥泥土的气味，还有床单的气味，在屋外风干后的新鲜气味。但还是很难看清东西。岛上没有路灯，没有街头广告牌的灯光，没有路过的汽车灯光。这种黑暗和寂静是你在城里完全体验不到的。这也是约翰喜欢这个小岛的原因之一。

但是现在当他醒来的时候，他感到不舒服。他不喜欢他躺着的这个房间这么黑。这让他感到紧张。他感觉有些不对劲。慢慢地，在黑暗中，他开始辨认出那些轮廓：浅色的是墙；深色的是别墅里沉重的家具——床尾的巨大衣橱，他们用来放衣服，甚至可以放上两倍多的衣服；墙上的油画是两个男人在沙滩上，正把他们的小船推进大西洋汹涌的巨浪中。

● 第76页

　　当他开始意识到自己在哪里的时候，他也觉得事情非常不对劲。房间里很安静，比起它该有的安静还要安静。他只能听到外面大海的声音，还有风从屋子的窗户中吹进来的声音。屋子里面没有声音。他伸手在床上摸索着找雷切尔，但手还没有触摸到冰冷的床单，他就知道她没在那里。他从床上坐起来，想要叫她的名字，但是什么也没有说出来。他努力想大喊，但是什么也没喊出来。他的呼吸又快又粗。他拽起床单，从床上扔了下去，发现床上还是什么也没有。他下了床，跑到衣橱那里，打开朝里面看。然后他跑到窗户那里，拉开窗帘。他看着外面的一片漆黑，把脸紧紧贴在冰冷潮湿的窗户上，默默呼喊着雷切尔的名字。他看到外面一个人也没有。他转身跑向帕特里克睡的小床那里，当他看到床上也是空无一物的时候，他再次试图大喊。

● 第77页

　　他跑到客厅里，推开、踢开挡他路的家具。他大声呼喊着她的名字，这次他喊了出来，这个名字是从他的心底里喊出来的，他用手捂住耳朵想要阻止自己的尖叫。当她不在这里的时候，当她离开的时候，听到她的名字让他痛苦万分。

　　他跑到前门那里，拉了拉门，但门纹丝不动。钥匙就在锁上，他转动钥匙。但是只是钥匙在转，门锁丝毫未动。他又跑回卧室，当他看到衣橱的门正在打开时，他突然停了下来。它慢慢地打开，有人从里面走了出来。是一个黑衣人。白色的脸庞成了屋里唯一的亮光。很难看出这是个男人还是女人。他手里拿着什么。他说话了。

声音是船上那个男人的声音。

"孩子很好。不要担心。"约翰看到那个男人正抱着帕特里克。

约翰想要说什么，但是他的嘴巴很干，一个字也说不出来，然而他听到了一些问题，就好像有别人在问。

"你在干什么……你是谁？你抱着我儿子干什么？……哪儿去了？"

"孩子很好，"那个男人说，"没事的，他现在会没事的。事实上他们并没有真的死去，你知道的，他们回来了。那些还不到时间就离去的小家伙们，他们会从另一边回来。他们总是会回到我们身边，他们总是会回来的。"

● 第78页

"什么！你在说什么？你是什么意思，回来？什么另一边？你在说些什么？你是说死亡吗？我的儿子很好，他没有死！你是不是疯了？而且……"约翰再次环顾了一下房间。"而且……我的妻子哪儿去了？你对我的妻子做了什么？"

约翰试图观察那个男人的脸，但还是很难看清任何东西。他注意到那个男人的头发很短，但这是他能看到的全部了。那个男人又说话了，声音温和柔软。

"现在她的工作做完了，她可以回到另一边去了。你现在可以让她走了。她做得很好。你看这个男孩儿，他很好。一个可爱的孩子。"

约翰看着帕特里克在那个男人的怀中睡着，便伸手去接他，但是就在伸出手时，他感觉自己开始向后跌倒。起初很慢，非常慢。那个男人依旧在说话。他的嘴巴在动，但是约翰再也听不见他说什么了。现在约翰感觉自己往下跌落得越来越快。但是那个男人依旧站在那里，似乎并没有离得更远。约翰全身都能感觉到自己在坠落，即使周围的一切都没有动。他再次伸出手臂，那个男人也伸出了他的手。虽然约翰仍在坠落，但是那个男人的手越来越近，最后触碰到了他的脸。一切都停止了，然后突然一切又陷入了黑暗。

第 10 章　没说出的梦和说出的梦

● 第80页

雷切尔弯腰看着约翰，抚摸着他的脸。他睁开了眼睛。他能看到她的嘴在动，但是什么也听不到，慢慢地他听见了她在说什么。

"约翰？约翰？你还好吗？我担心得都快疯了。你消失了好几个小时。发生了什么事？你看起来很糟。我害怕极了。我以为你出事了。你还好吧？发生了什么？约翰，跟我说说话！"

他的嗓子很干，他发现很难说出话来，但最后他还是说了出来。

"我在哪儿？帕特里克呢？"

他坐起来环顾四周。他还在水池边上。慢慢地他想起来自己在哪里了。此时太阳已经比他入睡时低了很多。

"我睡着了。我做了个梦。很可怕，一个可怕的梦，一个噩梦。很糟糕。我以为你走了，以为你离开我了。我找不到你。我到处找。太可怕了。天啊，太可怕了。那个男人抱着帕特里克。帕特里克！他在哪里？帕特里克在哪儿？"

● 第81页

"他很好。他很好，亲爱的。里根夫人正在照看着他呢。"

"里根夫人？"

"是的，你认识的，就是酒吧里的那个女人。他很好，他很好。"

她把他拉近自己，紧紧抱着他。她把脸贴在他的头发上，拥抱着他。她抱着他，让他尽情地哭。她以前从来没有见他这样哭过。

"我以为你走了，"他说，"我以为你走了。"

他哭着，一遍又一遍地重复着这句话。

她紧紧抱着他，过了许久，直到他的眼泪慢慢地不再流，尽管他全身还在颤抖。然后她慢慢地扶他站了起来，他们离开水池，沿着通往小岛另一边的小路走着，回到别墅那里。

他们走着，没有说话，但是她能感觉到他的体力正在慢慢地恢复。她不再帮他走路，只是用手挽着他的胳膊。现在她需要挽着他，就像他需要她一样。当他们走向别墅群和第一家酒吧的时候，他们转身面对对方。

● 第82页

"我以为我失去了你。"

"我以为我失去了你。"

他们同时说出了这句话。他们俩，同时说出了同样的话。然后他们扑向对方的怀里，拥抱着对方，这一次他们俩都哭了。他们这样站了很长一段时间。他们静静地站在那里，就像挂在当地一家酒吧里的画中人一样。那幅画中，一个男人和一个女人抱在一起，哭泣着，就好像他们其中一个人要离开很久，或许是永远。

这个小岛见证了很多这样的离别，因为男人们离开这里去英格兰或者美国找工作。他们许诺会尽快回来，或者寄钱给女人，这样她们就可以过去找他们。有时候钱会寄过来，有时候连封信都没有。

有时候男人会回来。

"我现在没事了，真的。"当雷切尔稍微往后退了一点儿，疑惑地望着他的脸时，约翰说。"真的，"他继续说，"那只是个梦。虽然是个很可怕的梦，但只是个梦而已。我没事，我没事。我想或许我比自己想象的要累一些。那只是一个梦。我没事了。真的，我没事。"

● 第83页

* * *

他们回到酒吧，找到了正在和里根夫人开心地玩着的帕特里克。

"啊，他是个可爱的孩子！是个小宝贝。我都想把他留在身边了。照看他真是件开心的事情。真的。你知道吗，下次你们来这里时，一定要住在酒吧里，我可以帮你们照顾他。"

"这里有房间吗？"约翰问。

"当然，你知道我们有房间的，约翰。"

"不，我是说，你们现在有空房间吗？下周要住的话？"

"约翰？我们明天就要回去了。"雷切尔提醒他。

"我知道，但我想或许我需要休息更长一段时间。我现在还不想回去。我可以打电话给办公室那边，告诉他们我要再休一个星期的假。你觉得怎么样？看看帕特里克。他多喜欢这里。在伦敦他可没机会看到这么多沙子和海水，是不是？而且他在这里很安全，是不是？没有车水马龙，什么危险也没有。拜托，你觉得怎么样？要不要留下？"

● 第84页

"但是在你……在那之后，……你确定在那之后还留下吗？"

"那是个梦，雷切尔，那是个很可怕的梦，但只是个梦。我最近做了几次噩梦，但那都只是梦，别无其他。我梦见我失去了你……"他的声音又一次近乎哽咽。他深吸了一口气，然后说完了他的话。

"现在我只想在这里再待一个星期，和你共度一些时光。我还不想回去工作。"

* * *

于是他们又在岛上待了一个星期，但不是住在别墅，而是搬到了酒吧，住进了酒吧上面的一个房间。这里确实比较吵，特别是在晚上。岛上的酒吧似乎想什么时候关门才会关门，而它们都是直到凌晨三点才想关门。但是帕特里克整夜都能睡着，而且比起安静，约翰现在更喜欢吵闹。他和雷切尔经常加入楼下酒吧里的人群中，一起唱歌，一起享受 crack，即爱尔兰人所说的愉快的交谈，里根夫人也很乐意照看帕特里克。

"比起听这些老家伙们唠叨，我更喜欢照看这个可爱的孩子。"她看着她的丈夫和他的兄弟说道，他们都在酒吧里工作，大家都笑了。

● 第85页

但是酒吧关门后，约翰依旧很难入睡，他讨厌在黑暗中醒来。这样他就会想起自己的梦。上床睡觉时，他会紧贴着雷切尔躺下，而不是像他们平时一起睡觉时那样背对着她。他喜欢紧贴着她来感受她的呼吸。

他们没有再提起他的噩梦。约翰不想提。他想忘记它，尤其想忘掉那个黑衣男人说的关于帕特里克和雷切尔的话。他想忘记这个梦，就如同他已经在努力忘记白衣搭车人的故事一样。他想忘记这一切。他只想抓牢他的妻子。他意识到这是在他们的婚姻中自己第一次有事情没有告诉雷切尔。他不喜欢这样，但是他不想谈起这些事情。

他躺在雷切尔身边，手放在她的肚子上，感受着她呼吸时的起伏。他不想放开她。他几乎害怕入睡。

不过，随着这一周过去，他开始放松下来，每次酒吧门打开的时候，他也不再紧张地向后看了。但是他不再单独出去长时间散步了。他们只是去一些很近的沙滩，帕特里克在那里发现了玩沙子的乐趣。约翰一直忙于不让沙子进到帕特里克的嘴里、头发里、眼睛里和身体的其他部位。他喜欢和儿子在一起共度时光，他向自己保证，将来要花更多时间陪伴帕特里克，少花点儿时间在工作上。

● 第86页

最后一天晚上，他和雷切尔一起去散步，把帕特里克留给里根夫人照看。这是这个假期中他们第一次不带着帕特里克一起外出。他们走到小岛的尽头，在那里，一艘巨大的渔船在十五年前被冲上了岩石。真是令人称奇的景观。这艘大船停在距离海平面五十米高的岩石上。自从被风暴困住、被海浪冲上岩石后，它就一直停在那里。

"很神奇，是不是？它就像一个巨大的玩具。帕特里克会喜欢这个的。"约翰边围着船走边抬头看着它说道，"他们没有钱把它弄回海里，所以就把它留在了这里。真是太神奇了。"

雷切尔在他身后轻声说话时，他还在抬头看着那艘船。

"我想跟你说说我的梦，在帕特里克生日前我做的梦。还记得吗？"

● 第87页

约翰点点头。

"我现在可以告诉你了。现在我们在这里了，而且他的生日也过完了。现在我觉得他安全了，你知道的。"

"你确定吗？"

"是的，我想告诉你。那个梦太可怕了，像你的梦那样，但是我现在想说说它。"

她坐下来，约翰坐在她旁边，他们的背倚着船的一侧，她开始讲了。

"我做这个梦三四次了。我梦见我和一个孩子在一起，但他不是帕特里克。他很像帕特里克，但不是他。我们正在准备他的生日会。他坐在我身后的地板上，玩着玩具汽车，发出各种声音，模仿着汽车的声音。我觉得非常开心。我的内心感到十分温暖，我知道我从来没有这么开心过，我自己哼着歌，微笑着……然后……"

约翰用一只胳膊搂住雷切尔，她朝他笑了笑并点了点头，但是这次的笑容来得不是那么容易。

"然后，"她继续道，"然后一切都变了。我突然觉得有些不对劲，我想转身看看他，但是我无法……我无法转身。我甚至不能扭过头看他。然后我意识到了我听到的声音不再是他的玩具汽车发出的声音。那不是他模仿出来的汽车响声，而是真的汽车声。突然周围黑了下来，我不是在屋子里了，我在……我也不知道我在哪里。然后汽车的声响越来越大，接着是一声尖叫和一声巨响，整个世界仿佛在不停地翻转，我看不到那个孩子了……后来我就醒了。我一遍又一遍做同样的梦，我变得非常害怕。我担心帕特里克会发生什么事情。我不知道是什么。但是我害怕汽车，我害怕靠近它们。我害怕在帕特里克生日前他会发生什么事情。我肯定在他的生日前会有不好的事情发生。太可怕了。但是现在没事了。他很安全。我们都很安全，是不是？现在一切都很好，是不是？那只是个梦，对吧？就像你的那个梦一样。我的梦并不意味着什么。你的梦也不意味着什么。是不是？"

● 第88页

雷切尔把脸埋在他的胸前，约翰搂着她，把她抱在怀里。

"现在没事了。"他说。

雷切尔看不见他的脸，看不见他脸上的表情。他的脸再次变得惨白，看起来很惊恐。他记起了那个警察讲的那起车祸，以及车祸中死去的婴儿；记起了那个黑衣男人说的关于婴儿"从另一边回来"的话；记起了那个男人讲的在布赖顿的路边遇到一个搭车人的故事。而现在雷切尔梦到了车祸中的婴儿！

● 第89页

"现在没事了，"他再一次说道，"没事了。"

但是约翰不确定他相信自己说的，他不确定相信自己的话。

第 11 章　停下！停下！

● 第90页

约翰站在家中的卧室里。那是星期天晚上。他们前一天从爱尔兰回来了，现在约翰要准备明天去上班了。上班前一天晚上，他总会把衣服准备好，这样第二天早上他就可以在床上多躺几分钟。在他不得不起床去上班以前，能多几分钟躺在雷切尔的身边感受那种温暖。他从衣橱里拿出了他那件深蓝色的夹克衫。他自己比着它，站在镜子前。这是他上班时经常穿的一件夹克衫。他看着自己。经过两周的假期，他看起来很放松，也被太阳晒黑了。

但是他并不觉得放松。假期中有那么一段时间他觉得很放松，但是雷切尔的梦把他所有的恐惧都勾了起来。关于那些梦，还有警察和录音中那个男人所讲的故事，有太多他无法回答的问题。这些问题他甚至都不想去思考，但是他无法忘记它们。

他从床边的桌子上拿起钱包，放进了夹克口袋里。口袋里已经有什么东西了。一个盒子。摸起来像是一个烟盒，但这不可能。他已经有十多年不抽烟了。但是他现在更希望那是一盒烟。现在他觉得自己想抽根烟，现在他觉得自己需要抽根烟。他从口袋里拿出那个东西，看了看。是个磁带盒。他打开它，里面有一盘磁带。磁带上什么也没有写，有那么一会儿，他在纳闷儿那是什么，然后他想起来了。

● 第91页

他上一次穿这件夹克是在最后一天上班的时候，珍妮和他开车去布赖顿的那天。这是他们在他办公室里听过的那盘磁带，来自一家电台，里面讲述了白衣女人的故事。他一定是在那个星期五他们离开办公室的时候把它放进了口袋里。

约翰站在那里，看着手中的磁带，那天的所有感觉现在又都回来了。他的嘴突然变得很干，他的心似乎跌到了谷底。

"约翰，晚饭好了。你下来吃吗？"雷切尔在楼下喊他。

"我马上下去。"他回答道。

● 第92页

他看了看手中的磁带，把它放到了床边的桌子上，但是又立刻拿了起来。他不想让雷切尔发现它。他把它又放回口袋里，下了楼。他想晚些再处理它。

他们一起吃了晚饭。他们吃饭的时候约翰很安静，但是这没有让雷切尔感到惊讶。假期结束的时候他经常这样。他喜欢自己的工作，但是他发现在假期结束后很难回到工作中去。假期结束后的最后一个晚上对他来说通常很难过，所以她没有对他的沉默说些什么。

　　他们很早就上床睡觉了，雷切尔像往常一样很快就睡着了。她总是睡得很好，但是只要帕特里克有一点儿声响她就会立刻醒来。今晚帕特里克睡得很安静。

　　然而，约翰却无法入睡。再次看到那盘磁带，使他想起了所有关于白衣女人的故事。他几乎能听到那个男人在他的脑海中讲述那个故事，讲着那个男人的故事，讲着约翰的故事。雷切尔静静地躺在他的身边。约翰没有像往常半夜醒来时那样伸出手去摸她。他的脑海中充满了画面，就像一部快进播放的电影，又像一部电影混合着另一部电影。雷切尔穿着一身白色衣服站在爱尔兰悬崖上的画面与讲述搭车人故事的话语交织在一起。雷切尔站在布赖顿附近一条偏僻马路上的画面与车辆碰撞的画面和声响交织在一起。画面中还有他们在爱尔兰的卧室，以及一个穿着黑色衣服的男人说的话，是关于帕特里克"从另一边回来"的话和"她的工作完成了，她现在可以回到另一边去了"的话。

● 第94页

　　约翰躺在床上越来越热。他的思绪不停地跳跃着，但是当他听到尖叫声时他立刻坐了起来，浑身变得冰凉。

　　他坐在床上听着。雷切尔没有动。他什么也没有听到，只有雷切尔平缓的呼吸声。他快速走到帕特里克的房间，低头看着孩子的床。帕特里克也睡得很香。他看了看窗外。没有人。其他人并没有听到任何尖叫声。尖叫声，就像那些画面一样，只充斥在他的头脑里。他站在那里看着帕特里克。帕特里克很安静，但是他安全吗？雷切尔安全吗？他慢慢地走到衣橱那里，像梦中那样打开了门。他翻遍了衣服。他不知道自己在找什么，或是在找什么人。那里都是衣服，只有衣服。

约翰走到另一间卧室，坐在床上，双手抱着头，闭着眼睛，试图不去看任何东西。

"这里到底发生了什么？我这是怎么了？我这是怎么了？我要疯了吗？这一切意味着什么？上帝啊，救救我，救救我。请救救我吧，我完全不明白这一切。"

他坐在那里，用手抱着头，轻轻地抽泣起来。

● 第95页

他一定是睡了几个小时，因为当他再次睁开眼睛的时候，天已经亮了。他洗漱了一下，穿好衣服，没有叫醒雷切尔。他没有叫醒她就离开了家。他没有像往常那样去抚摸她，也没有和她吻别。他只是坐进车里，开车走了。

慢慢地，随着他开车前行，他的思绪开始平静下来。白天的时候，事情似乎有所不同。前一天晚上的事情就像是另一个噩梦。他那最糟糕的恐惧感和焦虑感总是在半夜袭来。早上他回想起这一切，都不敢相信他自己的感觉和他在夜里做的事情。"这一切会有一个解释的。"他想。

他开始想着工作，心情开始好转。这是个美好的早上，约翰喜欢开车——清晨的美好可以驱散那些无眠之夜的可怕想法。他开始放松下来，期待着回到工作中去。他打开车上的录音机，按下了播放键。这是一盘录有他最喜欢的爱尔兰歌曲的磁带。正在播放的歌曲听起来非常悲伤。

希尔霍，爱尔兰

1890 年

179

我亲爱的、挚爱的儿子，约翰

很遗憾带给你

那么悲伤的消息

你那亲爱的年迈的母亲

已经去世了

我们在莫伊拉的小河边

安葬了她

在你那年幼的弟弟汤姆旁边

● 第96页

　　约翰开始轻声地抽泣起来。他想起了自己四年前去世的母亲，是在他遇见雷切尔之前。他仿佛看到了母亲的面容就在眼前，看到了那个为她举行葬礼的小教堂。他现在哭了起来，就像母亲去世时那样哭泣。他一边继续注视着前方的道路开着车，一边试图用手擦干眼泪。

　　就在他擦干眼睛的时候，音乐停了，取而代之的是那个男人的声音，他正在讲搭车人的故事，讲白衣女人的故事。约翰看了看录音机。一个男人的声音现在从里面传来，是电台节目中那个男人的声音。

　　我只想让她下车。我说："我们就快到那里了。"但是她没有回答。突然，我正接近一个道路拐弯处时，她开始尖叫。我的心一下子凉了……

● 第97页

约翰按下录音机上的停止键，但是那个声音还在继续。

……胃也猛地一紧，她在尖叫："天啊，我们要失控了，我们要失控了，当心，当心，天啊！"

约翰按下录音机上的一个按键，磁带弹了出来，但是那个声音还在继续。为了盖过这个声音，约翰开始大声喊叫。他不想再听这个故事了。

"停下，停下。我不想听这个。你听见了吗！停下，停下。我受够了！"约翰大声喊着，用左手拍打着录音机。约翰的眼睛里充满了泪水。那个声音还在继续。

……她也在看着我。她看着我……我很难描述那个眼神，但是……我不知道那是什么，好像她想要看透我是一个什么样的人。那是，我不知道，那眼神既性感又不确定，好像她不知道是否可以信任我。我的意思是，在眼泪和刚刚的一切过去之后，我感觉有一点儿兴奋和紧张，还有一点儿不自在。

● 第98页

约翰几乎看不清他前面的路了。

"停下！停下！停下！"他喊叫着，用左手胡乱地拍打着录音机。他的整个身体都在颤抖，他不停地喊叫着。

"停下！停下！停下！停下！我不想再听这个了。这不是关于我的。你明白吗？这与我无关。这不是我的故事。停下，停下！让我安静会儿。求你了。请不要来打扰我们！"

他身后的一辆车在按着喇叭，闪着灯。一辆朝约翰驶来的车也在闪着灯。约翰眼睛里的泪水使他几乎没注意到这些。然后他突然意识到那个声音停了下来，他也意识到自己的车正在疯狂地左右摇摆。他第一次听到了后面汽车的喇叭声，看到了朝他驶来的汽车闪烁的灯光。

他把车开到路边停了下来。一直跟在他后面的那辆车从他身边开了过去。司机朝着约翰看过去，并用手指指着自己的头，似乎在说："你疯了吗？"

约翰没有注意到他。当他把车停下来以后，他双手抱着头，开始号啕大哭。

第 12 章 不要回头看

● 第99页

约翰在车里坐了一会儿，然后开车去上班。他坐在办公室里，但是无法考虑工作的事情。他的电视节目的成功现在看起来都是无意义的。他回到车上，开车在伦敦转了几个小时。有一两次他看到了前往布赖顿的路标。他停下车，看着那些路标。他考虑过开车回到那个村子。但是天已经黑了，他决定还是回家。

他并不期望回家。当他到家的时候，晚饭已经做好了。吃饭的时候约翰很安静。

"你还好吗，约翰？你很安静。有什么事情吗？办公室发生什么事情了吗？"

"我很好，"他说，"你知道我总是觉得回去上班很困难。"

"你是在担心什么事情吗？自从在爱尔兰的最后一天起，你就一直这么沉默。要是有什么事情的话，你会告诉我的，是不是？约翰？你会告诉我对吧？"

● 第100页

"是的，当然。但是我很好。我很好。只是回去上班不太适应，你知道的。"

他站起身来，绕过桌子朝她走去。她以为他要吻她，但是他只是把手放在了她的肩膀上。

"我很好。真的。"

雷切尔很早就去睡觉了，但是约翰没睡。

"有个电视节目我想看看。"他说。

后来当他确实上床睡觉的时候，却无法入睡。他几乎是害怕睡着，害怕自己可能会梦到的事情。躺在雷切尔身边也让他感觉不舒服。他又去了旁边的卧室，稍微睡了一会儿。早餐时，雷切尔再次问他是不是有什么事情。他们以前在这个房子里从来没有分床睡过觉。但是约翰只是说他在想工作上的事情，睡不着。说没有什么重要的事，没有什么异常。

他们俩第一次意识到，他们之间有了一些无法说出口的事情。但是约翰不能多说什么。他怎么能告诉她自己半夜躺在黑暗中时，脑海里充斥着的那些奇怪想法呢？

"今晚我会工作得晚一点儿，"他说，"我昨天几乎什么也没干。你知道假期后第一天上班是什么样子的。我会晚点儿回来。不用给我准备晚餐了。"

● 第101页

约翰上了车，开车走了，但是他没有去上班。他再一次开车四处逛了几个小时，最后他选择了去往布赖顿的路，回到了那个他第一次遇见雷切尔的地方，也是那三个男人遇见搭车人的地方。

他在车里坐了几个小时，然后回家了。但是第二天晚上他又去了那个村子，然后，第三个晚上，他又回去了，坐在车里，在他第一次遇见雷切尔的地方。

第一个晚上他来到这里时，什么也没有看到。但是第二个晚上，在他车上的后视镜里突然出现了什么。约翰的头发都立了起来。他听到车子旁边有脚步声，但是他继续直视前方。随后脚步声继续前进着，他听到了狗的叫声。当一个男人牵着狗从旁边走过时，他松了一口气，但是那个男人停了下来。他回头望向车子，弯下一点儿腰，试图朝里面看。约翰摆了摆手，但是很明显那个人很好奇是谁在深夜独自坐在车里。那个人继续走着，但是几分钟后又从马路的另一边回来了。然后那个人开始横穿马路，朝着车走来。约翰迅速发动了引擎，开车走了。他不想跟那个人解释自己在做什么，他没有任何合理的解释。他确实不知道自己为什么要再次回来。

● 第102页

现在约翰第三个晚上来到村子坐在车里。这是个潮湿的夜晚，行程中一直温暖的车子现在变得越来越冷。由于他的呼吸，车窗内侧都起雾了，很难透过玻璃看清外面。他用夹克的袖子擦了擦玻璃。外面也没有什么可看的。道路在他的眼前延伸至山上，空无一人，漆黑一片。他前方没有路灯，他身后村子那边的路灯照不到这么远。道路前后都是空荡荡的。他已经在这儿坐了半个小时了，只有两三辆车从这里经过。他又擦了擦后视镜，打开了后车窗的暖风机。窗户开始慢慢地变得清晰，他可以看到外面了。他现在能从后视镜里更清楚地看到车后面的路了。从一些房屋里照出来的灯光加强了路灯的光。他可以清楚地看到他身后的第一个房子。前面的两扇窗户亮着灯，他觉得自己能看到有人坐在里面，但或许那只是件家具，或许是把扶手椅。他身后的其他房子都只是黑乎乎的形状，没有其他什么了。他冻得直打战，他问自己在这里做什么，为什么要一次又一次地回到这个村子。

● 第103页

　　他已经来这里待了三个晚上了。没有人来。没有白衣女人。她就是他期待的人吗？难道他认为她每个晚上都来这里吗，那个神秘的搭车人？如果她真的来了，如果她今晚真的来了，然后会怎样呢？好吧，那他就会知道，不是吗？无论如何他都会以某种方式知道。或者就像珍妮所说的那样，是一个正在寻找记忆的女人，或者……还可能是谁呢？雷切尔？难道他真的认为那会是雷切尔吗？难道他真的认为那个白衣女人就是雷切尔吗？

　　而如果这个白衣女人不来呢？如果没有人来，就像第一个晚上没有人来，第二个晚上也没有人来。然后呢？他会继续从伦敦开车穿过半个城市来到布赖顿停下车等待，一直等到另一个村民看到他并报警吗？要在这里等多少个晚上呢？如果一直没有人来，那意味着什么呢？这真是疯了，完全疯了。这根本无助于他回到正常的生活中去，这会毁了他的，这会……

● 第104页

　　后视镜里出现一抹白色。他起初以为那是道灯光，然后他仔细看了看后视镜，但是白色还在那里。那是裙子的白色。一个白衣女人。一个白衣女人就站在他的车后，一动不动。他只能看见她身体的一部分。他看不到她的腿，看不到她的头或脸。因为她站的位置，他只能从后视镜中看到她的一部分。他不想回头去看她。他很害怕。

他从侧视镜里看了看，又能多看到一点儿。是的，一个女人，肯定是个女人。但是他还是看不见她的头和脸。他现在感觉车内更加冰冷。他的胃顿时变得很空。他的手感觉好像粘在了方向盘上。他动不了，她也没有动。然后突然她朝前走了一步，约翰看着她从后视镜里消失。他从侧视镜里看到她又朝前走了一步。"噢，天啊，这是怎么回事？"他轻声自言自语道。

那个女人朝前移动着，然后在车旁停了下来，停在副驾驶座的门旁边。约翰转过头看了看。那条裙子现在很靠近窗户。当她伸手去拉车门把手时，他听到一声响动。把手动了动，但是门上了锁，约翰没有去开那个门。她的手抬起来搭在了车窗上。是她的右手。他看了看她的手。晒黑的修长手指上没有戒指。她伸出一个手指，似乎要敲车窗，或者是要在潮湿的玻璃上写些什么，然后那只手挪开了，她也往后退离了车子。她缓慢地移动着，所以透过车窗可以看到她更多的身体。她又朝后退了一点，他可以看到更多，然后她又退了一步，约翰可以看到她的脖子，然后……

● 第105页

约翰在没开车灯的情况下行驶了差不多一公里。他发动了引擎，就在那个女人后退的时候，车子向前蹿了出去，他目视前方，疾驰而去，沿着路开出了五百米后，他才意识到自己在做什么。

他没有回头看。他不打算回头望这条路了，也不会去回想过去一个月左右发生的任何事情。他告诉自己，这是他最后回想自己在岛上的那个梦。他不想失去他的妻子。他不会失去他的妻子，他当然不会因为自己过去几个星期以来的疯狂想法而失去她。

● 第106页

他继续行驶着。路上没有别的车。在这样一个漆黑、潮湿的夜晚，他开得比安全速度要快很多。现在似乎和在爱尔兰的别墅时一样黑，和他梦里的场景一样黑。

他用了不到二十分钟时间从村子里开出了快三十公里，此时他从后视镜里注意到了什么，好像是从车的后座上发出的光。他放慢车速，回头看了看后座。

他的手机在后座上，光是从它那里发出的。手机。他可以给雷切尔打电话。她应该在家里。他又想起了那个他不想看到其面容的白衣女人。那是二十分钟前的事了。那个女人不是雷切尔。雷切尔在家里。他现在就可以给她打电话，她会接的。他把车停在路边，拿起了手机。

他坐着盯着它看了一分钟。即使是像他开得这样快，也得再花半个小时才能到家。没有人能从那个村子开车现在就到了他家。这不可能。他现在可以打给雷切尔，她会在家里，这样他就会知道那个白衣女人是别人了。然而，他只能坐在那里，看着手机，恐惧再次袭来。

● 第107页

然后他拨通了家里的电话。电话响了，没有人接。电话继续响着，然后他听到了一个声音。那是他自己录在答录机里的声音。

"很抱歉，雷切尔和约翰现在都不在家，无法接听您的电话，如果您想……"

他的眼睛里再次充满了泪水，他几乎无法呼吸，然后突然，答录信息停止了，他听到了雷切尔的声音。

"喂……"她的声音带着睡意。

"雷切尔？"

"约翰？你在哪里？你还好吗？电话响的时候我在睡觉。"

"我很好，亲爱的。我正在回家的路上，大约半个小时后到家。你会等我吗？"

"我当然会等你。"

"雷切尔？"

"嗯。"

"我爱你。"

"我也爱你，约翰。快点儿回家吧。"

"我会的……我会的。"

他发动车子，踏上了回家的路，在到家之前，他是不会回头看的。